KARATE

AN INTRODUCTION TO COMPETITION KARATE

BLANDFORD

DEDICATIONS

Bryan: I dedicate this book to Bill Winfield, a friend and fellow karateka who is sadly missed.

Ronnie: To Mrs M. Hegarty and Mrs E. Christopher.

ACKNOWLEDGEMENTS

I have received a great deal of support from many friends and students in preparing this book. With sincere thanks I acknowledge their kindness. I would in particular like to thank:

Dr Peter M. Flowerdew for his merciless editing, his time, encouragement and friendship; Johnathan Flowerdew for his enthusiasm and versatile keyboard skills; Chris Jackson for his help in printing out the draft manuscript; Bob Poynton for his inspiration, continued support and invaluable advice; Dawn Gunby for her excellent drawings; Adrian for being Ronnie's opponent in the illustrations; David T. Hewitson and Bob Roberts for their terrific photography. Finally, a very special thanks to Tracy for amusing Alexander so that I could write – I really ought to marry her some day.

PHOTO CREDITS

Bryan Evans: p. 6.
David T. Hewitson: pp. 26, 61, 70.
Bob Roberts: 14, 21.

Front cover: Frank Brennan utters the *kiai* 'spirit shout' as he scores on his opponent in the KUGB National Championship at the NIA, Birmingham.

The publishers are grateful for the help of Paul Clifton of *Combat* magazine for providing the cover image.

A Blandford Book
First published in the UK 1995 by Blandford,
a Cassell Imprint
Wellington House
125 Strand
London
WC2R 0BB

Distributed in the United States by Sterling Publishing Co. Inc.
387 Park Avenue South,
New York, NY 10016–8810

Distributed in Australia by Capricorn Link (Australia) Pty Ltd
2/13 Carrington Road, Castle Hill, NSW 2154

British Library Cataloguing-in-Publication Data
A catalogue record for this book is available from the British Library

ISBN 0 7137 2556 7

T96 8153
Ev 15g

Design and computer page make up by Tony and Penny Mills

Printed and bound in Great Britain by The Bath Press, Avon

CONTENTS

FOREWORD

It brings a great and special satisfaction to an instructor when they are inspired by their own students. I have long felt this inspiration from Bryan, in the observation of his performance of karate and in the display of his obvious grasp of the fundamental principles of karate as a science and as an art. I was therefore more than pleased to hear that he had decided to use his abilities to examine and publicize the considerable talents of Ronnie Christopher.

Ronnie is truly a remarkable exponent of the art; his technique and attitude never fail to inspire and for many years he has been a wonderful ambassador for British karate. As an international competitor he has excited karate enthusiasts the world over with his unique and spectacular style of fighting. In one way he was highly unpredictable: he would attack or defend, kick, punch or sweep, or frequently blend techniques in a continual variety of combinations until he found his target. However, in another way he was highly predictable because every technique was characteristically performed with total commitment, awesome ferocity, absolute control and exemplary sportsmanship.

With this book, Bryan has also 'found his target'. Books on competition karate have appeared on the market over the years, but unfortunately few have done more than describe the start and outcome of a series of karate clashes, omitting the process of training and tactics that allow them to be executed with effectiveness. This book does indeed 'get to grips' with the details and the objective way in which it is structured makes it a highly useful manual for those who wish to aspire to greater success in their competition career, or for those who are simply curious as to how it is done by a real expert. No doubt other experts could have emphasized different points, or put the same point in a different way, but I doubt if any will disagree with its contents – I feet that this is a book which will prompt a whole new series of healthy debates and articles.

I would certainly recommend this book to all practising karteka. I would also recommend it to those who do not practise but are interested in finding out about 'real' karate. This book is, as I would have expected, devoid of any hint or mention of the almost 'superhuman' powers so often falsely attributed to karate practitioners and which have created fantasy images which began in the 1960s with James Bond and continue today in the form of television series such as *Power Rangers*. This work represents an accurate account of a real karate expert's reason for success, and emphasizes the importance of training scientifically, regularly and earnestly if this success is to be emulated. It is a book which, I am sure, could be read, appreciated and enjoyed by top athletes from any sport or discipline, and presents karate in a deservedly good light. It is a product of two outstanding members of a new generation of British karateka, and is a reassuring sign to the preceding generations that they have certainly done something right.

BOB POYNTON

6th Dan, Senior Instructor
to the KUGB

Chairman of the Technical
Committe of the English Karate
Governing Body

INTRODUCTION

Most karate students have some difficulty in translating the skills acquired through basic training to the more challenging free-style sparring. Formal, pre-arranged sparring drills have been developed to accommodate basic techniques, but problems can arise in trying to make these techniques work in the unstructured free-style sparring required for *shiai*, the contest. More seriously, this could indicate an inability to apply karate for its original purpose, an effective method of self-defence.

To assist the student, this book presents practical, easy-to-follow drills that will help the karateka to make the transition to free-style sparring. It will be emphasized that this transition does not involve sacrificing the principles of this powerful fighting art. Whilst free-style techniques may only be a part of the total repertoire of karate, it is important to avoid the misconception that competition fighting is a dilution of the art or that its techniques are not effective.

The powerful, rapid and accurate techniques demonstrated with great skill on the competition mat will be effective in any situation. Anyone who has seen Ronnie Christopher in action will have no doubt that his skills would be more than adequate for self-defence purposes. The practice of karate involves the systematic training of the whole body, together with the development of the character, to enable an unarmed person to defend themself as if they were actually carrying weapons. The karateka who trains earnestly in basic technique will develop fundamental principles essential for sport and self-defence. Effective self-defence requires more than knowing a few useful techniques; it also requires honed reflexes, speed, focused power and, in particular, a strong, determined attitude. Given the quality and severity of training undertaken by most élite karate athletes, it is no surprise to find that they have acquired these qualities, because they are essential for both the mat and the street.

The drills and ideas presented here should provide the reader with clear and specific objectives for their training, and will hopefully assist in exploding the myth that competition karate is not *true* karate. Even if entering competitions is not the aim of the reader, there are many benefits to be gained through training diligently in this way which can only enhance the karateka's overall ability.

(OPPOSITE) Ronnie regularly uses 'active' stretching methods during personal training. Here, he holds out a fine example of *yoko-geri kekomi*

1 THE HISTORY OF SHOTOKAN KARATE

The birthplace of modern karate is, surprisingly, not mainland Japan, as is popularly believed, but the distant southerly island of Okinawa, the largest island of the Ryukyu group, which lie east of mainland China. For centuries the islands were ravaged by civil wars and subjected to military occupation from both China and Japan, which led to considerable social and economic unrest. Successive feudal regimes banned the carrying of weapons, so unarmed combat flourished, taught deliberately by way of obscure, ritualistic forms, to ensure that deadly techniques remained secret. Systems of weaponless fighting had been a feature of these islands for generations and included methods assimilated from Chinese and South-East Asian origin, as well as their own indigenous systems.

The martial arts of the Far East contain tried and tested methods of extraordinary diversity and complexity. They have survived generations, being passed only by demonstration from master to student. This has left a unique legacy from an age when this knowledge was a matter of life or death. An important factor in assisting the survival of this knowledge has been the close links that have been created between karate and the traditional culture of Japan.

Shotokan karate is a modern system derived from the much older Chinese and Okinawan unarmed combat systems. It was introduced to the Japanese mainland in 1922 by its founder, Gichin Funakoshi, a 53-year-old schoolteacher. He is generally regarded as being the 'father of modern karate', although there were many other masters living at the time who had their own ideas, and the styles that they taught still flourish today. Funakoshi ensured his historical prominence, however, by his timely introduction of the art to the Japanese. So popular was this 'new' art that Funakoshi was persuaded to remain in Japan. It seems he never returned to Okinawa, but lived the remainder of his life developing and promoting karate throughout the mainland.

Funakoshi, who had studied karate all his life, had initially referred to his art as 'Chinese hands' (kara – Chinese, te – hands), but later altered the way the first character was written to mean 'empty', although it was pronounced the same way. So the literal translation for 'karate' be came 'empty hands'. This removed the association with China, which contributed to its acceptance by the Japanese during a time of intense nationalism.

Funakoshi recognized that in order for karate to be fully accepted by the martial art fraternity, it had to be presented in terms of the philosophy underlying all the existing classical Japanese martial arts. This philosophy is expressed as Bushido, literally 'military-knight-ways', usually expressed as 'the Way of the Warrior'. It is a complete ethical code embraced by the Samurai class of old, which balanced the freedoms of power with the duties of the protector and gave Samurai warriors the courage to face death fearlessly and is closely related to our Western concept of chivalry. The roots of Bushido are in the national religion of Japan, Shintoism. This supports a practical philosophy embodying such attributes as loyalty, courage and virtue. To this were added aspects of Zen Buddhism, which taught the transitory nature of life, created the calm stoicism that maintained composure in the face of danger and the art of concentrating totally on the present moment, *zanshin*, a state of awareness that will be discussed later.

The fighting systems that had existed on Okinawa were practical, battle-tested self-defence methods and held little or no allegiance to moral or ethical concepts, being simply *jutsu* – deadly fighting techniques. Funakoshi was keen that his 'noble art' should officially be recognized alongside other Japanese *budo* (martial ways) and so he added the suffix *-do*, meaning 'the Way', to place it alongside such arts as kendo, the Way of the Sword, and aikido, the Way of the Spirit. The deadly Okinawan art of karate was instilled with a moral conscience, exemplifying such things as courtesy, good etiquette and self-control, to become karate-do, 'the Way of the Empty Hand'.

Funakoshi became friends with Jigoro Kano, the founder of judo, whose interest in karate probably contributed to its widespread acceptance by the Japanese. Kano had first seen Funakoshi's karate when the Okinawan was invited to give a demonstration at the Kodokan (judo hall), and it is possible that they influenced each other. Certainly their philosophical outlook was similar, for Kano was transforming jujitsu to judo in the same way that Funakoshi was creating karate-do. They were concerned that their students should cultivate virtue and a mature outlook on life, and learn to avoid conflict outside the dojo. The fighting arts were to become a means of developing character as well as physical skills.

Funakoshi and his assistants continued to promote karate in various educational institutions and in particular the universities. This was a vital factor in the development of the art. Like judo and kendo before it, karate was subjected to the scrutiny of scientific study to improve and refine its techniques.

Funakoshi's teaching at this time consisted only of *kata* ('forms') and the *kumite* (fighting) that related directly to the application of the *kata*, because he considered them to be the essence of karate-do. Younger instructors and students began to engage in some pre-arranged sparring, *yakusoku kumite*, but it appears that *jyu-kumite* (free fighting) was considered too risky. This was in the days before the concept of control was formulated.

It was not until 1938 that the name Shotokan emerged. Shoto was the pen-name Funakoshi used for the poetry he wrote as a youth. It meant 'pine waves' and derived from his love of walking on cool evenings in the foothills of Mount Torao in Okinawa and hearing the pine leaves rustling in the breeze. It was during moments like these that Funakoshi experienced a meditative state and was able to reflect on the spiritual aspects of his art. The name Shotokan was originally the title given by his supporters to Funakoshi's first dojo in Japan. Shoto-kan, translated, means 'the Hall of Shoto'. Over the years the 'style of the Shoto-kan' became 'the Shotokan style'. The opening of this hall, or dojo, in 1938 heralded the official birth of Shoto-kan karate-do.

Funakoshi's son, Yoshitaka, was an extremely powerful, athletic and talented karateka who further developed the art. His youth and vitality give rise to a new approach, in which he introduced lower stances and the concept of involving the whole body in each technique, the hallmarks of modern Shotokan. He also introduced the additional kicking techniques of *mawashi-geri*, *yoko-geri* and *ushiro-geri*, particularly with the head as a target. Up to that time kicks were usually aimed only at the knee and hip joints and other low targets. When the great master was too old to be fully involved in teaching at the Shoto-kan, he appointed his son as the chief instructor. Despite contributing so much to the style, Yoshitaka is seen as a comparatively obscure karate pioneer, possibly because he died quite young, before his 40th birthday. There are different views on the cause of his death, though he had suffered from tuberculosis all his life and most probably died of pneumonia.

During World War 2, karate practice was dispersed and it was not until some time afterwards that the masters regrouped to work at building its future. Master Gichin Funakoshi, now an old man, was a tremendous inspiration for the younger generation. He was a potent symbol and wrote the first books ever published on karate, his most famous being *Karate-do Kyohan*.

In 1949 the first national karate organization was formed, the Japan Karate Association (JKA), with Gichin Funakoshi as honorary chief instructor. This marked the start of an explosion in the popularity of the art, beginning with the interest and enthusiasm of occupying American military personnel. Recognizing the effectiveness of this art, the American services incorporated it into their unarmed combat systems. Funakoshi died in 1957 and his grave is marked with the epitaph '*Karate ni sente nashi*' – 'There is no first attack in karate', summing up his belief that karate was first and foremost a defensive art, with the perfection of the character being its primary aim.

Following the death of Funakoshi, Masatoshi Nakayama took over direction of the JKA, and through this organization Shotokan established itself as the most popular style of karate. Nakayama was a personal student of Funakoshi and had studied kendo before entering Takushoku University. The JKA became a national educational body under the Ministry of Education in 1955. Following this, Nakayama and his assistants formulated the first grading structure for karate. Masters such as Hidetaka Nishiyama, Teryuki Okazaki and Kimio Ito were assistant instructors at that time and in 1956 they began special courses for instructors, the first students being Kanazawa, Takura and ami.

The first JKA championship was held in 1957 and Hirokuzu Kanazawa became the first champion. This event proved to be a turning-point in the history of Shotokan karate. Interest in the sporting aspect of karate quickly grew, although some people had reservations about this development. Many old masters rejected the idea that karate-do could be practised as a sport, fearing that the spirit of *budo* would be lost. Masatoshi Nakayama recognized this danger, and sought to reconcile the differences between the two approaches. He realized that in order for karate to grow and develop, and, more importantly, to be accepted by the West, it would need to adapt. Japanese instructors established that Westerners were strongly motivated by competition and that this had to be a part of what was offered to students. His strategy would seem to have been a success because under his guidance the JKA has grown into the most powerful karate organization in the world, with an estimated 10 million students in over 65 countries!

Grandmaster Nakayama died of a stroke in 1987. This led to political unrest within the JKA, which has still not been completely resolved. This kind of conflict is not new; the JKA has a turbulent history. Many prominent instructors have left to form their own associations. To a certain extent this is to be expected as people develop their own ideas and these new associations have probably contributed to the further growth and popularity of karate. Whatever the future may hold, Masatoshi Nakayama will be remembered as one of the most important karate leaders in recent history, a key figure in the dissemination of karate around the world.

In the early 1960s, the graduates of the famous instructors' class – Kanazawa, Kase, Shirai and Enoeda – toured many countries throughout the world. They visited the USA, where Nishiyama had settled, and Europe. Keinosuke Enoeda had already travelled extensively before the JKA sent him on one of these world tours. He had visited and taught in Indonesia and also stayed in South Africa for a year. Sensei Kanazawa was given the task of developing karate in the UK in 1965, and became chief instructor of the

newly formed Karate Union of Great Britain. The KUGB was created with many of the clubs from the old British Karate Federation, which had been formed in 1959. Sensei Kanazawa taught mainly in the south of England whilst his assistant, Sensei Enoeda, moved to Liverpool to teach. Within a year, however, Kanazawa resigned as chief instructor of the KUGB and moved to Germany. Sensei Enoeda then took over as chief instructor. With his senior students, Sensei Enoeda has built the KUGB into the premier karate organization of the UK.

Master Enoeda began karate when he attended Takushoku University. Having practised judo as a boy he quickly became a powerful karateka. He began training after seeing a karate demonstration at the university and within two years he had gained the prestigious black belt. Among his many instructors was the Grandmaster, Gichin Funakoshi. Enoeda became captain of the university team and was then accepted into the JKA instructors' class. This was an intensive three-year course under the guidance of Masatoshi Nakayama. During this time Enoeda was able to train with many famous karateka, including top sensei from other styles of karate. He was nicknamed 'Tora' (Tiger) by his colleagues at the JKA because of his immense power and fighting spirit. He won the annual All-Japan Championship in 1963, beating his friend and rival Hiroshi Shirai, who had defeated him in the finals the previous year.

After Kanazawa's departure from the KUGB, Enoeda decided to continue teaching in Liverpool. This was a key decision for the future success of karate in the UK. He started instructing full time at the Liverpool Red Triangle with a unique set of students. Those now famous students, Andy Sherry, Terry O'Neill and Bob Poynton remember with great fondness (and a little fear) those early days when the shaven-headed Enoeda drove them to their limits, and then a little further, during harsh training sessions that have passed into legend! Master Enoeda was intent on providing the kind of training he had experienced back in Japan. Many young people must have left at the sight and sound of this fearsome-looking Japanese, whose only desire seemed to be to kill them! But for the likes of Sherry, O'Neill and Poynton, men of tougher fibre, Master Enoeda was just the inspiration they needed.

It is fitting that the Liverpool Red Triangle, the birthplace of the KUGB, produced so many prominent karateka. Undoubtedly one of the most famous is Frank Brennan. He dominated the senior individual *kata* and *kumite* event in the National Championship over a period of 14 years. Throughout his illustrious career he won many top international honours, including Grand Champion of Europe and the World Kata Crown. In 1980 he received a special award from the late Grandmaster, Nakayama, for his outstanding perform-ance. One of the highlights of his career was being the captain of the KUGB squad that defeated the formidable Japanese national team at the World Championship in 1990. The coach to the Japanese team, Masahiko Tanaka, who is himself an ex-World Champion, paid homage to Brennan by admitting that he was the one man that the whole Japanese team had been specifically trained to beat. It is doubtful whether Frank Brennan's record of successes will ever be equalled, such was his extraordinary ability. He retired from competition in 1992 after once again becoming Grand Champion, and the undefeated KUGB Kata Champion for 14 consecutive years! During his reign, he epitomized all that is admirable in competitive karate, displaying not only the power and exemplary technique that set the standard for all aspiring karateka, but also the dignity, courtesy, respect and good sportsmanship that are hallmarks of the *true* karateka.

There have in the past been many multi-style karate governing bodies whose purpose it was to co-ordinate and monitor the many different organizations in the UK. Unfortunately, in many ways there was only an illusion of control, which resulted in further division and ill-feeling. This was due in no small part to the skilful manipulation of certain 'karate politicians' who abused their position to further their own aims and not those of karate-do. The chaos that this unfortunate state of affairs led to, in which it seemed that just about anyone, regardless of their credentials, could officially set themselves up as a 'master', was finally brought into focus when the Sports Council conducted its own investigation into the management of karate in the UK. The result of that inquiry, in 1986, was a report which over-turned many stones and led to the setting up of the English Karate Governing Body (EKGB), which is now working hard to bring about unification, promote high technical standards and define good prac-tice for all karate clubs throughout the UK. A national coaching package for EKGB instructors is being examined which should ensure uniform standards in coach-ing and instruction and a major step forward for karate in the UK.

2 A PROFILE OF RONNIE CHRISTOPHER

'The Samurai', a title once given to Ronnie Christopher by the late karateka Steve Cattle, is a fitting description that sums up Ronnie's tremendous fighting spirit. Whenever he approaches the mat, his face becomes a mask of concentration, and with the referee's call of *hajime*, he assumes an awesome *kamae* (ready position). His determination and courage are an inspiration to everyone, certainly befitting his comparison with the legendary warriors of old Japan. His dedication to the art of karate goes even deeper than would be apparent from his many national and international successes and has earned him the high esteem and respect of senior instructors.

Ronnie has always been a sports enthusiast. Even as a youngster he would throw himself whole-heartedly into any physical activity, oblivious of any danger. He once tried to teach himself gymnastic skills but had to give up because, without proper tuition, he was constantly falling and hurting himself. He has a passion for playing football and demonstrated an ability that could have led to a professional career. Fortunately for us, this natural athlete fulfilled himself through the practice and study of karate and was not distracted by more lucrative, but perhaps less deserving, sports.

It is interesting that Ronnie first saw karate whilst playing football in the school gymnasium. On one memorable occasion, Ronnie recalls that a friend forgot to bring his 'trainers' and could not join in the game. He instead stood barefoot at the sidelines, and, becoming bored, started to kick the wall with his toes, or so Ronnie thought. He was so amazed at the sight of this that he forgot the game and quickly went to investigate, convinced that what he had witnessed was something magical. His friend proudly replied: 'I'm practising my karate.' Ronnie learned that his friend was using the ball of his foot, a natural weapon, and not his toes as he had first imagined. But that only interested him further and from that moment on Ronnie's ambition was to find out more about this intriguing art.

The result was that Ronnie joined a local karate club, along with several other friends. Suddenly he had found something that truly inspired him, something that was both mysterious and physically challenging. That first club practised Shotokan karate, as Ronnie recalls, but did not belong to a mainstream organization and within four or five months it closed. Looking for another club, Ronnie tried various styles of karate but did not find one that suited him until he came across a friend who had started at the original

National Championship 1993, National Indoor Arena, Birmingham. Ronnie narrowly misses his opponent's head (R. Watkis) with a back round-house kick in the opening moments of the hard fought finals. Sensei K. Enoeda 8th Dan, chief instructor to the KUGB, presides over the match.

Shotokan club with Ronnie, and was now training at another club. Ronnie clearly remembers his friend's excitement at describing the karate he was now practising, which was the familiar Shotokan. But that was where the similarity ended; there was nothing familiar about the training which was, according to his friend, very harsh and dangerous.

This rather ominous description captivated Ronnie's imagination and motivated him to attend the new dojo (training hall). He immediately realized that here was an approach to karate totally different from anything he had experienced before. There was an air of discipline and deadly seriousness pervading the dojo which was clearly reflected in the concentration and determination mirrored on the faces of the students, amplified by their *kiai* (spirit shout), as they attacked and

defended with vigour. Ronnie felt a sense of foreboding which mingled tantalizingly with his desire to experience at first hand the karate he was witnessing. At once it was apparent to him that what he had been practising all those months was not true karate, but a mere imitation, lacking the spirit of the true art. Instinctively, he knew he had found authentic karate. The instructor was a formidable, unforgiving but very impressive karateka who was fully involved in his class. The young Christopher had walked into the dojo of the KUGB's Cyril Cummins, a senior instructor of considerable experience.

Ronnie was determined to enrol and start training just as soon as he gained permission from his mother. He hurried home excited, full of enthusiasm and anticipation, impatient to tell her of the good news that he had finally found a club that practised realistic karate. He obviously had not accounted for the effect that this would have on his mother. She had come to recognize that Ronnie was the type of boy who could be quite reckless and who therefore needed careful guidance and a measure of restraint to ensure that he came to no harm. Ronnie's enthusiastic and detailed account of what he had witnessed only served to alarm his mother to the degree that she promptly decided that the club was far too dangerous. Anxious that he should participate in a less aggressive sport, or concentrate on academic pursuits (she was a schoolteacher), she did not agree to his joining. Not so easily dissuaded, the young Christopher demonstrated his tenacity by ultimately convincing her that no one ever got hurt in karate, and that there were rules and regulations that he would have to follow to ensure this. With that assurance, she eventually allowed Ronnie to join the club. Once he enrolled, his natural ability soon asserted itself, but it was his single-minded determination to push himself to the limit, with the help of his instructor of course, that accelerated his progress. He started to enter competitions and, not surprisingly, also started to win.

In those days, anyone placed in the last eight in a KUGB event would be invited by Sensei Andy Sherry, the national team coach, to attend three squad sessions for assessment and possible inclusion in the national junior squad. The age range for this squad was, and still remains, 16 years to 21 years. Ronnie recalls vividly those early selection sessions. Nothing he had done before prepared him for the challenges he faced at the Liverpool Red Triangle. The very name of this dojo still causes ripples of apprehension in the minds of anyone familiar with the legendary exploits of its famous senior instructors.

There is a hint of pride in Ronnie's tone when he describes his feelings and memories of those days. With some humour he muses on the strange experience that whenever he bowed at the door and crossed the threshold, no matter how bright and sunny it was outside, once inside the dojo everything seemed to become dark and grey. All personal problems had to be left at the dojo door so that his mind was clear to cope in surviving the ensuing hell. Everyone training on those sessions quickly found out that they would be driven to their physical and mental limits. Any egos that may have fed on the success of winning a competition or two were soon deflated under the relentless barrage of flying fists and feet and the ever-watchful eye of Sensei Sherry. Anyone who had delusions of grandeur found the squad sessions a very unfriendly place indeed. All were treated as equal, regardless of track record or ability. Having ability alone was no insurance that a student was capable or worthy of representing his country. Sensei Sherry has always looked deeper, in search of other, more sublime qualities.

One thing that Ronnie Christopher will always emphasize during his teaching is mental attitude, and how this affects the performance of karate. Without it, karate is just a superficial exercise. It is probable that most people train superficially in karate. Karate will have a profound effect on the personality and character only if it is undertaken in a very serious manner, in which the karateka is able to confront fears, and overcome physical and mental barriers. Ronnie is emphatic in underlining the importance of training in the correct way, whatever the student's grade. Just as beginners may struggle with basic movements, higher grades must endeavour to impose challenges on themselves that force them to struggle in the same way as do the novice grades. He says that it is so easy, having gained the black belt, to stagnate and not really train hard at all. As proficiency in technique increases, and the execution of the movement becomes less demanding, these challenges are more mental than physical.

Training in the junior squad emphasized these challenges. There was a constant danger of injury, forcing everyone to confront their fears, with many falling at the first hurdles. Real tears were shed during those sessions, but some of those who did the crying went on to become accomplished national squad members and outstanding karateka. Those who came to the Red Triangle with any ideas of 'showing off' and basking in the kudos afforded by being part of the British national team quickly decided that, despite perhaps their having ability, there were easier and far less painful things to do. For those who survived, however, their karate underwent a metamorphosis that elevated them above the average karateka.

Without doubt, to attend squad sessions then, and now, demands a great deal of courage. Weeks before, Ronnie admits to having experienced a fleeting state of panic at the mere thought of attending another session. With typical determination he was able to overcome his fear and insecurities, which would increase significantly prior to every session. Despite his feelings he never missed a session. He is adamant that training on those sessions was instrumental in improving not only his karate, but also his character. Without the fear, sacrifice and sheer hard work he experienced during those early years, and the guiding influence of Andy Sherry, he is confident that his life would have taken a quite different, less positive course.

People who dismiss the competitive exploits of our leading karateka would do well to recognize that the men and women demonstrating their skills have bravely endured extremely hard trials which have forged their characters in a way that accords with the philosophy intrinsic in true *budo*.

Ronnie Christopher is a product of this process, a true *budoka* (one who practises and lives the martial arts) who upholds the true spirit of karate-do. He continues to spread the word of karate and brings his considerable experience to his teaching, a true ambassador for the art of karate. Ronnie has been teaching in his own clubs in and around Birmingham for a number of years and has produced many successful competitors, winning regional and even national events. He has recently accepted the position of coach to the northern area squad.

Listed below are just some of Ronnie's achievements. Whilst he has been placed highly on many occasions in *kata* events, his most notable success has been in *kumite*:

Junior European Individual and Team Champion

Senior European Individual and Team Champion

KUGB National Individual Champion, three times

World Team Champion, twice

Silver Medallist, World Championship, twice

EKB (English Karate Board – All Styles) National Champion, three times

EKB National Team Champion, four times

KUGB Shotokan Cup, National Individual Champion, three times

3 CODE OF BEHAVIOUR

It seems that some organizations professing to teach karate do not recognize the need for a code of behaviour. They treat karate as only a sport, removing it from its context as a fighting *art*. Instructors of such organizations can legitimately teach potentially dangerous skills to young people without accepting any obligation to infuse them with a sense of responsibility. The pitfalls of this approach are clear: they could be producing skilled playground bullies. The instructor bears the responsibility for creating a person with fighting skills, who must also have the appropriate strength of character to ensure that those skills are not abused. Ronnie's own story illustrates just how the attitude of an instructor can have a profound impact on a student, together with the positive effects of dojo etiquette and discipline. Many parents report improvement in their children's behaviour upon joining a suitable karate club. The disciplined attitudes they pick up in their training are also often translated into their approach to school work.

The traditional karate dojo etiquette has developed from that of the other Japanese martial arts, especially the Way of the Sword. The master swordsman would be careful in choosing a student, often testing their character first. The training environment had to be well structured and disciplined, not only to avoid accidents,

but also because the student had to learn self-control. This served the dual purpose of instilling in the student not only the ability to fight with a clear mind, should conflict be inevitable, but also the option to avoid the inappropriate use of violence. To be goaded into using their skills was regarded as the greatest possible weakness of character. These concepts are just as valid today as they were in feudal Japan, and it is to emphasize this that true karate keeps the obvious and clear links to its traditional roots – even to the extent of using the Japanese vocabulary.

The code of behaviour originally formulated by the Japan Karate Association has been adopted in various forms by the major karate organizations world-wide. With typical Japanese brevity it addresses behaviour towards fellow students, instructors and conduct outside the dojo.

> **DOJO CODE:**
>
> Exert oneself in the perfection of character
>
> Be faithful and sincere
>
> Cultivate the spirit of perseverance
>
> Respect propriety
>
> Refrain from impetuous and violent behaviour

These expressions address *attitude*, from which appropriate behaviour follows. Genuine karate clubs should have some code of conduct which all karateka, regardless of rank, should follow closely. The rules given below as an example are those of the EKGB.

1. Bow on entering and leaving the dojo.

2. Address any instructor as 'Sensei' whilst in the dojo.

3. 'Oss' is a sign of respect and is used generally in karate especially in the following situations:

    (a) Upon receiving any advice or command from the instructor, the student must reply by answering 'oss'.

    (b) When bowing at the start and finish of the class.

    (c) When bowing to your partner during *kumite*.

    (d) In any other appropriate situation, for instance during gradings or competitions.

4. Train at least twice per week.

5. No one is to leave the class without first obtaining the permission of the instructor before the start of the class.

6. Any member arriving late must take up a kneeling position at the front of the dojo and await permission from the instructor before joining the class. On receiving permission, bow and then join the class.

7. Fingernails and toenails must be kept clean and short.

8. Gis must be kept clean and in good condition.

9. Jewellery (rings, bracelets, neck chains, etc.) must not be worn during training. If you can't get a ring off then tape must be wrapped around it.

10. Apply for a licence *immediately* upon being accepted into the dojo, so that personal insurance cover can be obtained.

11. Members must not smoke, chew, spit or commit any other act likely to offend the etiquette of the dojo.

12. Members must not use their skills in any offensive way outside the dojo.

It is the responsibility of the club instructor to ensure that all students abide by the rules of the dojo and conduct themselves in an appropriate manner. Senior students must recognize that they will by virtue of their rank be viewed as role-models by junior grades and particularly children, therefore it is imperative that behaviour is exemplary.

Certain behaviour can clearly show whether a student has a poor attitude. For example, some students bow to their partners in a very offhand manner, or refrain from moving about the dojo with any urgency, particularly when asked by the instructor to change partners. In any situation where students are asked to line up, such as with the commencement and finish of the class, or when students are summoned to 'circle' the instructor in order that finer points can be more clearly shown, it should be done quietly and quickly.

It is advisable for students to pay careful attention to the instructions given by the sensei at all times. It is often a habit of higher grades to 'switch off' when they consider the instructor to be imparting information of a basic nature. This is a serious fault, which can convey a lack of respect. The instructor should be observed at all times by everyone in the class, as there is always the possibility of seeing what was perhaps missed before. If you are not instructing, then regardless of grade you are the student and should accept that role and behave accordingly. Provided that the teaching content of the class is clear and unambiguous, there should be no problem in following the advice given. It is important that instructions are followed *to the letter* and that a personal interpretation does not occur because this could impair learning and even put other members of the class at risk.

There is nothing worse for an instructor than to have to try to motivate a class of people who look as though they would rather be somewhere else. An instructor is entitled to take the view that because the student has paid their fee and changed into their *karate-gi*, they must be willing and ready to undertake instruction and train in the correct spirit. The student who will not train in this way is probably wasting their own and the instructor's time. It is only natural that the instructor will give most attention to those students who are enthusiastic and attentive.

The emphasis on good attitude and good behaviour is relevant to all situations, including the competition arena. The competitor must always display good conduct and self-control. Respect for one's opponent is paramount, beyond any concerns over victory or defeat. The competition arena should be regarded as an extension of the dojo, the atmosphere being one of dignity and reflecting the serious intent of the karateka.

A danger of sport karate is that its winner's podium can provide a platform to elevate an already over-inflated ego. Having 'defeated' all opposition, the successful competitor may consider themself above criticism. In extreme cases they may even believe themself to be masters of the art of karate, the implications of which are obvious. Young people, unable to keep their success in perspective, are particularly prone to this temptation. This is why the karate instructor bears the responsibility for much of the student's development as a person, and why a martial art should never be regarded as merely a sport or game.

4 THE THREE Ks:
KIHON, KATA AND KUMITE

Traditional karate parallels other forms of *budo* in that it consists of three distinct areas of practice. To ensure optimum progress, all three disciplines should be studied with equal emphasis. The three Ks will now be described and the way in which they complement each other will be discussed.

KIHON (BASICS)

Kihon is an area of practice directed towards the acquisition and development of the fundamental skills which *kata* and *kumite* training will need to build on. Ideally, a student should not participate in any form of *kumite* or attempt *kata* until these basic skills have been acquired. The practice of *kihon* develops specific skill in stances, basic blocking, punching, kicking and striking techniques, and, allied to this, training for developing good posture, co-ordination, balance and speed.

In practising *kihon*, students perform set drills with many repetitions. As the student progresses, the movements become more complex, enabling the student to build up a vocabulary of techniques which will, in time, become natural to perform. The key to development is constant honing and repetition, determination and a conscientious instructor or coach who will be able to spot mistakes and help the student eradicate them before they become set. It is worthwhile remembering that it is the *quality* of technique, which is important, not the quantity.

The practice of *kihon* is often likened to the foundations of a house. They are the building blocks. It is no use having the finest furniture, fabrics and wall coverings if the house is in danger of collapsing. Lacking solid basics, a karateka's ability will be seriously flawed, even ineffective.

Apart from the practising of basics being a means of assimilating technique, it is also an effective method for strengthening the whole body. Without prior conditioning, karate training can be abusive to the body when performed at full speed and power. This is sometimes apparent when an experienced karateka returns to training following a period of inactivity. If they train too enthusiastically to begin with, they may find that there is a price to be paid for decreased fitness, made evident by sore joints and muscles. So not only do basics programme the body to function in precise patterns, they also provide a tailor-made fitness routine, an important reason why their practice should always be a part of karate training.

KATA (FORMS)

Past masters have asserted that *kata* are the heart and soul of karate. Indeed, any

National Championship 1993, NIA. On this occasion Ronnie's punch almost cost him the championship. The slightest error in judgement can have the most devastating results.

combat system which does not include the practice of *kata*, despite any claims to the contrary, cannot be considered true karate. A *kata* follows a defined performance line, the *embusen*, and comprises a set sequence of defensive and offensive movements which are practised as a solo exercise, but with the attitude that opponents are attacking from all sides. Included in each *kata* are a wealth of self-defence techniques, many of which are forbidden in contests because they include attacks to vulnerable areas of the body which would be difficult to control in a free-style context.

Kata provide a unique method for keeping alive a legacy of tried and tested lethal combat methods. Many cultures have lost indigenous fighting techniques because they were no longer needed in everyday life, but the existence of the *kata* has prevented this from happening to karate. Approximately 60–70 *kata* are still practised in modern karate. Distinguishing one *Ryu* (style of karate) from another is made possible by examining its *Kata*. The Shotokan style comprises 27 *kata*, ranging from the simple *kihon kata* and the basic *heian kata* to those like *unsu*, which require the utmost skill and athleticism. The five *heian kata*, originally called the *pinan kata*, were developed by an Okinawan karate master, Ankoh Itosu, who was one of Gichin Funakoshi's teachers. The *kata* are very old, many originating from China, though they have been modified extensively over the years.

There are two styles of *kata*: those of the *shorei Ryu*, which emphasize power and strength, and those of the *shorin ryu*, stressing light, quick movements. The former style of *kata* is said to suit better the person of a large build, whilst the latter are designed for the smaller person. In practice, however, all *kata* must be performed with the correct application of power, agility and speed. If it is assumed that one *kata* is for those who are more powerful or quicker and lighter, then this can lead to an erroneous performance and an inhibition in learning a *kata*; a karateka may dismiss a particular *kata* with the excuse 'it doesn't suit my build'. It may be of interest to *Kyu* grades that all the *heian kata* are considered as *shorin-ryu kata*.

Important considerations when performing a *kata*:

1. You must bow at the start and finish; which signifies courtesy.

2. *Kata* must be performed with a demonstration of martial spirit and awareness.

3. Breathing should be harmonious with technique.

4. The *embusen* should be adhered to.

5. You should have understanding of the techniques within the *kata* and a clear idea of the target area.

6. Correct use of force is important, tension in the muscles at the wrong moment dissipates energy and interferes with the correct application of force.

KUMITE (SPARRING)

This practice, of its nature, involves the use of a partner. There are a great many variations of *kumite*, ranging from the formal five- and one-step pre-arranged sparring drills to free-style. Formal basic sparring involves applying, as the name suggests, the *kihon* (basics) to attack and defence with an opponent. It provides a valuable opportunity to test one's proficiency with all the offensive and defensive techniques, with the extra challenges provided by the elements of timing, distance and accuracy.

Basic one-step sparring, *kihon ippon kumite*, is frequently regarded as being the closest to the feeling of applied combat in a self-defence situation. This is primarily because the defender does not assume a free-style *kamae* or defensive posture in anticipation of the attack. Instead, the defender remains in natural stance, whilst the attacker steps back into *gedan-barai* (downward block) and nominates a target area to be attacked. That target will then be attacked vigorously, with the defender using his skills to block and then immediately counter-attack. Practising in this way perhaps corresponds more closely to the type of situation that might occur on the street, in that it follows the principle that there may be insufficient time to assume a defensive posture prior to an attack. Both partners should strive to develop good balance, posture, timing, accuracy and speed, which must be backed up by a strong spirit. To ensure optimum development, the defender should feel as though they are really under threat, that unless they block or evade, serious injury could result.

A modification of this type of sparring in order to bridge the gap to free-style is to practise snapping-back counter-attacks. As the partner attacks, the defender blocks with either one of the basic techniques or a more advanced open-handed block.

They then counter with a punch that is immediately snapped back to *kamae*, as is usual in free-style.

Practising in this way also allows the defender to counter more rapidly against kicks, because in the usual basic format the defender has to delay their counter until the partner has landed so that they can focus and hold the counter-punch to the target. Unfortunately, waiting for the opponent to land may interrupt the necessary smooth flow from block to counter. By snapping the counter-punch, it can be made immediately, even if the attacker is still moving in towards the defender. One important point: the student must take care, when making the transition from thrust punches to snap punches, that they continue to involve the whole body, especially the hips, in each technique. It is easy to hide weak technique behind the snap punch, relying too much on the arms, shoulders and upper body.

The next stage is to progress to semi-free-style, *jyu ippon kumite*. The combatants assume the *kamae* (ready position) and are permitted to move about as they wish. When they do this, the distance between the opponents becomes a vital factor. It changes constantly as the fighters manoeuvre for the best position from which to attack or defend, and now the attacker must recognize and act upon the instant that the distance and angle suits their nominated attack. This form of practice is usually pre-arranged, though as the students' skill develops, attacks can be made without prior nomination. Following each attack, which should be extremely vigorous, the attacking arm is snapped back, or, in the case of kicks, the leg is rapidly withdrawn, to allow the quickest possible return to *kamae*. The attacker is not entitled to block the defender's counter-attacks. This is to allow the defender to develop fine focus and control.

When all the previous methods of sparring have been properly developed, then free-style sparring can be practised. This involves the free exchange of techniques with no one assuming the role of attacker or defender. Practice should always be conducted with regard to the safety of the partner. Sparring can be practised lightly or with full power. It can also be restricted to attacking or defending only with specified techniques. For example, one partner may kick whilst the other concentrates on delivering punches.

5 KEY ELEMENTS

The following topics deal with elements that are applicable to *all* karate practice.

KIME: THE FOCUS OF POWER

The key to being able to impart tremendous shock impact to a target is to combine physical and mental focus at a single instant in time. The body is naturally able to produce enormous energy utilizing mechanical principles but usually most of this energy is lost because of an inability to direct it usefully. The novice karateka will perform karate in a relatively unco-ordinated way, unknowingly pitting one part of their body against another, struggling to generate as much energy as possible but only producing a mass of muscular contradictions. With training, this energy can be harnessed and channelled to the appropriate part of the body, such as the knuckles when punching or a particular part of the foot when kicking.

Physically, *kime* relies on the instantaneous rapid, forceful contraction of the major muscle groups; principally the abdomen, the buttocks and the primary muscles involved in the technique. The rapidity of muscular contraction generates speed but also enables the body to apply the brakes to bring about a sudden stop to any movement. Being able to abruptly stop a technique, aids in the transference of energy to the target, resulting in the destructive power that is characteristic of true karate. Physical strength is an attribute which can only be fully exploited in karate by associating it with speed. It is the combination of speed and strength that produces power and it is this which must be focused, in a split second, to achieve *kime*.

The mental aspect of *kime* involves your being 'as one' with the technique, meaning that there should be a harmonious connection between the body and mind. Karate techniques should not be used casually, but should involve one hundred per cent commitment. The intention behind every kick or punch should be to end a confrontation without the need for further action. Closely related to this is the expression in karate '*ikken hissatsu*', 'to kill with one blow', which illustrates graphically that techniques used correctly have the potential to destroy an opponent. Without *kime*, the essence of karate is lost and it is in this respect that the late Master Nakayama, when considering sport karate, had the greatest reservations. He upheld the principle that karate should not become a superficial display of technique, lacking *kime* and therefore integrity and sincerity.

KOKYU: BREATH CONTROL

It is no mistake that karate is sometimes called 'the Way of Breathing and of Empty Hands'. When you perform karate vigorously, your rate of respiration will increase dramatically. This is because the body is normally in a state of oxygen balance in which the oxygen content of the blood equals the oxygen used by the muscles, but when you commence karate training the heart starts working harder, increasing the oxygen flow to the muscles to provide them with energy.

For the body to function at its optimum during hard exercise, the circulo-respiratory system (heart and lungs) has to adjust to cope with the increased workload. This is usually achieved in dojo training by a brief and gradual warm-up before intensive training. This is the ideal way to commence any vigorous activity. Karate, however, is a martial art and should be instantly usable in any situation. It would be rather inconvenient to have to warm up in order to deal with a threat faced on the street. In those first few moments of all-out action, the greatest demands are placed on the body's ability to function effectively. In a 'life or death' situation, the 'flight or fight' reflex, causing adrenalin to be released into the bloodstream, is an automatic reaction to stress and prepares the body for instant action. This, very effectively, replaces the need to warm up in situations of extreme stress or anxiety and explains why karateka are able to perform in competition without the need for a lengthy warm-up.

You should recognize the sensation of the 'fight or flight' response, not as a weakness, but as a sign that the body is preparing for action. However, this does cause an increase in your respiration rate, and you should try to control your breathing so that it is co-ordinated with your movement. Breathe as naturally as possible but exhale sharply with your technique. This contracts the muscles of the abdomen, enabling you better to apply *kime*. Think of each inhalation following a technique as similar to reloading a gun so that you are always ready to fire again.

Allied closely to breathing in this way is the *kiai*, or spirit shout. Although it is often said that the *kiai* must accompany maximum effort, it is not necessarily so. The *kiai* is used for two purposes: as a loud piercing shout it vocalizes your martial spirit, boosting your self-confidence, while secondly it can be used for effect to unsettle your opponent at a critical moment, giving you the advantage. Your breath control should be the same whether or not you actually utter the *kiai*, nor should there be any difference in the power or effectiveness of your technique.

ZANSHIN: 'TOTAL AWARENESS'

Zanshin is an almost meditative state of mind relevant to all the martial arts. It produces a detachment from intellectual processes so that reactions will be natural, instinctive and appropriate. Mastery of *zanshin* enables the martial artist to free the mind of distracting thoughts such as of winning or losing, ensuring that focus on the opponent never falters. It demands that full alertness be maintained, even during moments of seeming inactivity. A contest between two equally matched fighters is a test of *zanshin*, a psychological duel which can easily be lost should one or the other display the slightest weakness in attitude or concentration.

It is one of the most elusive qualities to

A past National Championship at Crystal Palace, London. Ronnie demonstrates his remarkable kicking ability.

be attained and can only be developed and maintained through regular, hard training. *Zanshin* is only possible when the *budo-ka* has acquired confidence in their ability to apply the techniques at their disposal. The novice student will have initially to concentrate the mind on the mechanical performance of a technique. Once proficiency is attained, the student no longer has to struggle with the technique and can direct complete attention to the opponent. Training in karate involves a constant process of honing new skills in an atmosphere of mutual co-operation between partners and then a testing of those skills under more stressful conditions, as in free-style, where *zanshin* becomes essential.

TELEGRAPHING

Being able to score points against a skilled opponent depends very much on your ability to deliver techniques without superfluous preliminary movements, because these would immediately betray your intention. In particular, habitual movements preceding your attacks should be avoided. These can easily be read by a sharp-eyed opponent, especially if they know your style of fighting. Even a change of expression or a deep and obvious intake of breath prior to launching an attack can be a costly mistake.

You should always assume that your opponent is capable of retaliation at any time. They may be waiting for you to make the first move, with the intention of closing the distance and beating you to the punch. Or they may be a skilled defender, who is able to block and counter decisively, even under severe pressure. For this reason, unnecessary movements prior to attack and defence are best avoided during free-style, except where such movements are designed to deliberately mislead the opponent. Students are taught in *kihon* that techniques have an origin (preparation), delivery and completion, with each aspect being of equal importance. The study of human movement, biomechanics, often concludes that for optimum efficiency preparation is a necessary part of the technique. For example, all the basic blocks involve a large preparatory movement – an indispensable part of the technique, so far as basics are concerned.

In free-style there is often not enough time to employ such methods, because you have to react instantly and appropriately to lightening-fast attacks. To try to do so would almost certainly invite a quick defeat. Together with the requisite preparation, basic techniques are significant in that they usually involve the entire body in only one action at any one time. For example, if you block using *age-uke* (rising block), you will typically position your hips, torso and arms to commit yourself fully to fulfilling the objective of that movement. Fundamental karate technique is characterized by this total involvement in a single movement, which does not always translate to free-style fighting.

There is a rather amusing tale often told by the legendary Terry O'Neill which illustrates graphically, by his own admission, the error in selecting an ill-chosen basic technique during free-style. In his first-ever competition, Terry was almost hospitalized by a kick to the throat. At the referee's call of *hajime*, he had stepped into *zenkutsu dachi* (front stance) and *gedan-barai* (downward block). The opponent feinted with a front kick to again draw Terry's downward block, and converted to a round kick to score the decisive point. His account, rather than demonstrating any lack of fighting skill, highlights Terry's ignorance of the rules at that time and illustrates lucidly the importance of not permitting the opponent any advantage. Terry O'Neill is justly credited with having been one of the most feared competitors of his day, but in that first competition he had no idea how to apply his technique in the competition arena. Of course, the very able Mr O'Neill did not allow this initial defeat to deter him and went on to win many honours in national and international competition.

In addition to responding appropriately to your opponent, you will improve your chances of scoring dramatically by developing an explosive start to every technique. The word 'explosive' conveys exactly the style of movement you should try to use. An explosion is something that happens very suddenly, with no warning, and produces devastating results. Your techniques should be comparable, being so sudden as to catch your opponent before they have any chance of reacting. They should not be aware of the start of your technique; it should seem to appear out of nowhere. You must train for an explosive start by working your techniques from a static stance, as you would for demonstrating basics in the *Kyu* grading. Especially, work at not giving away any indication that you are about to move; there should be absolutely no build-up or superfluous movements. Once you have acquired the skill to move sharply from a static position, it will translate easily to the more fluid free-style movements.

6 TECHNICAL PRINCIPLES

KAMAE: THE 'READY POSITION'

A *kamae* is the fighting stance that you will adopt with *hajime*, the referee's call to begin fighting. Adopting a *kamae* means much more than being physically ready; it also requires *zanshin*. Posture is important in the practice of karate, particularly with the *kamae*, which must radiate confidence. By constantly shifting between an offensive and defensive posture, the *kamae* can be used effectively to unsettle an opponent. Great fighters all have unique *kamae*. As you gain experience you should experiment with different postures, but the *kamae* referred to here – which you should start with – is a 'free-style' stance based loosely on *fudo dachi* (rooted stance). A slight bouncing motion with the weight being shifted constantly forward and back is used so that with added footwork, distance from the opponent is never fixed, unlike in basic sparring. This motion can also help in disguising the initial thrust of the attack as it is easier to accelerate once movement has begun than by trying to move quickly from a static posture. Both knees should be slightly bent so that the stance feels flexible and not rigid as in the *kihon*. The arms will be held with hands usually loosely closed, in a guarding position in front of the body so that the forearms 'aim' at the opponent, primed in readiness for punching. The *kamae* is illustrated in Figures 1 and 2.

All the attacking and defensive movements described in this book will start from this *kamae*. It is important to note that on completion of any punching technique, the hands are generally immediately snapped back to the ready position, in contrast to *kihon ippon kumite* (basic one-step sparring), where punches are held to the target.

USING YOUR HANDS

The use of the hands in karate competition is restricted to attacks requiring the closed fist, the open hand being used only in blocking techniques. Many of the techniques included in the *kata* are forbidden in contests because they involve specialized attacks directly to joints and vital organs which are simply too dangerous. Regrettably, this entails a loss of many of the more effective, traditional techniques of karate, but only so far as competition is concerned. Dojo training should compensate for this deficit by including the practice of as many diverse techniques as possible, not only to improve

FIGURE 1: An example of a *kamae,* or ready position. All techniques described in this book start from this *kamae.*

FIGURE 2: The same *kamae* as in Figure 1, seen from the front.

co-ordination but also so that the 'flavour' of the martial art is never lost. Every student should be aware that what they are practising is an ancient art and a skill which carries a great responsibility, a skill which if abused can result in the serious injury or even death of an opponent. It is therefore of the utmost importance that young people who intend to enter competitions recognize that karate is not just a sport, but is much, much more.

Hikete, or retracting the opposite hand, is common to most karate techniques involving the hands and should already be familiar to the karateka. All basic karate punches and strikes commonly utilize the co-ordination of both arms simultaneously. As one arm delivers the technique, the other is pulled rapidly back to the body – usually to the hip. This has the effect of balancing the technique and adding power, creating a feeling of simultaneously pulling and pushing. Pulling your opposite hand back quickly provides a faster, therefore more powerful, thrust in the attacking arm. Failure to employ *hikete* correctly can lead to a weakening of technique.

Hikete also has a very practical application. It simulates the action of grasping an opponent and pulling them onto your attack, enhancing its effectiveness. In its basic form, a punch such as *kizami-zuki* is held fixed at the target on completion, the opposite fist having been retracted and held in place on the hip. However, there are no fixed positions in free-style, so *hikete* is co-ordinated with the attacking arm so that both arms are quickly snapped back to the *kamae* position. Despite the high velocity at which punches are thrown, withdrawing the opposite hand will momentarily expose the body to counter-attack. The action of *hikete* undoubtedly makes for a more powerful punch, but at a cost. To overcome this, most experienced fighters are able to deliver techniques either with the use of *hikete*, at a decisive moment, or to use the opposite hand to simultaneously block. We suggest that you practise the drills in this book using both methods.

Most punches you use in competition free-style should conform to the principles of the basic *choku-zuki* or straight punch, regardless of the method of delivery, whether it be by stepping, thrusting the stance, twisting the torso or even jumping. The elbow controls the delivery of the punch. To ensure that attacks are as straight as possible, keep the elbow directly behind the fist at all times. Think of the elbow as pushing the fist on delivery of the punch and pulling the fist with the retraction of the arm. The arm should act like a piston, driving the fist in a straight line from *kamae* directly to the target in a smooth, rapid action, and returning along precisely the same route.

The illustrations in this book generally show the left foot forward stance but, even if you have a preference for training on one side, it is recommended that equal practice is undertaken on the opposite side to ensure balanced development and all round ability.

The following routines are not exhaustive and consequently it must be emphasized that there are a great many other variations, too many to include in this text. It is recommended that you study all the methods of attack and defence described here before engaging in any practice with a partner.

USING YOUR FEET

A karateka who has mastered *keri-waza* (kicking techniques) can deliver extremely powerful attacks with the feet. The legs are designed to support and transport the weight of the body, so they are much stronger than the upper limbs and can deliver correspondingly more powerful attacks. They are also longer than the arms, providing a superior reach. They are therefore ideal weapons to use against an opponent who is moving in to punch or grab from some distance, and they can be devastating against an unskilled attacker.

A problem with using kicks is the need to stand on one leg, which demands more than just static balance, requiring the karateka to compensate for twisting and thrusting movements. There is also the need for an appreciation of Newton's Third Law. This states that for every action there is an equal and opposite reaction and is quickly appreciated by any beginner trying to kick a shield or pad held by a resolute partner who has taken up a rooted stance. To their astonishment, they find themselves catapulted backwards, illustrating that they have not fully understood the nature of the forces involved in delivering a kick!

Over the past couple of generations, the art of kicking has evolved to a degree of skill probably unknown during the time of the old masters. Modern science, including biomechanics and exercise physiology, has helped the karate athlete of today to develop kicking techniques to a level never seen before. It is now commonplace to see the top competitors using their feet with the same ease as they would their hands. Ronnie Christopher is a fine example of an athlete who is able to do just this.

Defeating an untrained attacker by using your feet is one thing, but dealing with a trained karateka is quite a different prospect altogether. The first problem is that kicks are slow compared to techniques using the hands so to use them effectively requires a high level of skill. Even if you are very fast with your legs, a proficient opponent will be able to spot the basic kicks and select an appropriate counter-attack in a fraction of a second. Kicks have been modified to beat the skilled opponent by providing as little information as possible about the type of kick being used, until it is far too late to react appropriately. This has been achieved by beginning the three basic kicks – front, side and round-house kick – with the same movement. From *kamae*, the rear knee is lifted high in front of the body with the leg being fully bent so that the heel approaches the buttock. The support foot remains pointing forward and the arms are maintained in the guarding position. From here it is possible, without pausing, to execute any of the three basic kicks by pivoting, thrusting or a combination of both, through the supporting foot. The trick is to start your movement by lifting the knee and not by moving the upper body or the arms in any way that would reveal your intention. For example, a common mistake in using the side kick is to start the movement, prior to lifting the knee, by turning the front supporting foot outwards and twisting or leaning the torso away as the knee comes up. This immediately signals the nature of the kick to the opponent.

It will be apparent that the style of the round-house kick, *mawashi-geri*, is quite different from that which is taught in the 'traditional' style. In the latter version, the knee is first raised high to the side and then in a continuous motion is swung horizontally around to the front where, at the last moment, the leg is extended and the target is struck by the ball of the foot with a snapping action. The problem of attempting this style of kick against a similarly trained opponent is that there is a very noticeable and distinctive start to the technique, with the knee moving to a position in which it would be very difficult to do any other kick than *mawashi-geri*, but there is also a tendency for the torso, and particularly the head, to lean forward as the knee is raised to the side, offering a tempting target for a sharp opponent.

It is therefore as a matter of necessity rather than by choice that the round-house kick has been somewhat abbreviated. However, it will be apparent that this economical style is a worthy substitute and is capable of delivering an extremely powerful blow in any situation.

The American full-contact star Bill 'Superfoot' Wallace developed a similar, economical way of delivering his three tournament kicks. Using only his left leg (he damaged his right knee in his early competition days) he was able to outsmart his opponents by keeping them guessing as to which kick he would use. He could use equally well the side kick, the round-house kick and the back-hook kick *ura-mawashigeri*. They all began by lifting the knee high to the same position, which made it impossible to determine which kick was coming! His famous speed and extreme flexibility meant that he was able to deliver very sharp, heavy blows with his foot, often knocking out his opponents, who simply did not see the kick coming.

Many karateka do not have the flexibility to perform, with any success, the high and fully extended kicks often employed by the top competitors. It is essential to realize that without good flexibility in your hips and legs, you cannot achieve reach. Try this simple experiment after a thorough warm-up; have a partner stand to your side as a target. Stand erect on one leg whilst raising the other towards your partner, as high as possible. You can assist the stretch by catching your leg and using your arm to lift it in a side kick position. Notice the height of your foot in relation to your partner. If they are standing upright, of similar height to yourself and your foot is in front of their face, then you have good flexibility in the hips and legs.

But is it good enough? The evidence would tend to suggest that you have sufficient flexibility to kick head height without too much discomfort. Look again. Your mechanical position, in which your support leg is vertical with your centre of gravity being directly over the foot, enables you to raise your other leg quite high. But now ask your partner to grasp your ankle, supporting the weight of your leg, and slowly move away from you. Notice what is happening? Within a very short distance, you will find that you are really struggling to maintain your foot at their head height. The further they move away from you, pulling your centre of gravity towards them, the lower your foot moves.

What this means in terms of *actually* kicking is that in order to kick to head height with any effect, you will need to be standing quite close to your opponent. Increase the distance and you will have real problems in trying to kick to their head, unless their stance is very low. Remember that kicks work best at long range, before an attacker is close enough to lay their hands on you. To attempt to kick when range dictates that a punch or

strike should be used is asking for trouble.

I have sparred with Ronnie Christopher on many occasions and one of the aspects of his astonishing ability that has always, quite literally, struck me is his incredible kicking reach. Just when I thought I was out of the way and safe – he would kick me. I have joked at such times that he is actually in possession of a pair of telescopic legs!

It is this kind of flexibility that affords you reach and allows you the freedom to use truly long-range kicks. Unfortunately you have to invest a lot of time in its development. If you want to become a good kicker, there are no short cuts. But it is time well spent. The final chapter in this book will deal with this topic.

The kicks contained in this book are described in their basic form, but also with emphasis on practical aspects: their application in actual combat. Many textbooks deal with the subject of kicks by describing their basic form, breaking the technique down into several static positions. Emphasis is placed on the development of the mechanical proficiency of the various movements, often with little regard for other considerations. Whilst this approach is invaluable for developing basic skills, it neglects to address the forces that act within the body during complex movement and the effects transmitted back through the body on impact. These forces all conspire to distort the *prescribed* form as required in the static positions. What usually happens is that anomalies occur between the kick as it is established in the 'step-by-step' way and how it is *actually* applied in *kumite*. An obvious example would be the *ushiro-geri*, or spinning back kick. There seems to be a plethora of ideas on how the kick should be most truthfully constructed in the static positions.

This failure to reconcile both versions of the same kick, so that practice is consistent, was clearly demonstrated recently in a training session hosted by Sensei Bob Poynton 6th Dan, when he asked several black belts, including myself, to line up and demonstrate *ushiro-geri*, by the count; that is, as a series of static positions. Each person's interpretation of how the kick should start differed quite considerably, although we all claimed to be performing the same kick. These variations could not be explained in terms of being adapted to different strategies, as each person was supposedly demonstrating the same basic form.

Who was right? In the event no one was able to offer an interpretation of what the kick might *really* look like if it were possible to stop it at each stage. In fact, the 'step-by-step' interpretation bore very little resemblance to the way in which each of us *actually* performed the kick. This would seem to indicate that a lot of time has been invested in developing quite inappropriate and irrelevant skills. The method by which I had constantly tried to hone and improve my back kick was having exactly the opposite effect. My 'step-by-step' interpretation was at odds to the true and natural performance of the kick.

This underlines the need for correct technique in action to be studied very carefully and clearly understood. A golfer looking to improve their swing would soon realize their method is in error if they continued to slice the ball. They would then take the trouble to analyse their method. The confirmation that they are hitting the ball correctly would be that it will land where they intend. In karate, we do not have the benefit of being able to assess our performance accurately, unless we were actually to make contact. In basics we must rely on perfecting a method that we hope will achieve our objectives. What we do when we constantly kick the air is what a golfer does when they take a practice swing. The difference is that they have the advantage of being able immediately to put their swing to the test by actually hitting the ball.

This shows that when skills are practised in a broken down or 'step-by-step' form, they should as far as possible conform to the *correct* technique as it is expressed in movement. A simplistic analysis of techniques which is contrived because it has no respect for the constraints of physics as applied to the human body in movement must be avoided. Just like an athlete in any other dynamic sport, the karateka should strive to break skills down in such a way that they remain faithful to the actual technique.

You should now understand how important it is to test the effectiveness of your techniques by actually hitting something like a pad, a heavy bag or *makiwara* (striking post). The real meaning of good technique will soon become apparent. Even if your form looks correct and feels satisfying to perform, the chances are that when you hit that heavy bag for the first time, it will cause you to re-assess the basics you assumed had unlocked your hidden power. Until you do this, your karate may as well be another form of exercise, bearing only a superficial resemblance to something that could otherwise be considered a complete martial art.

7 COMPETITION TECHNIQUES:
YOUR ARMOURY

The reader should already have some knowledge of the basic stances, punches and kicks. This chapter will briefly describe the most commonly used techniques and how they can be adapted to the *kumite* match, both in attack and in defence.

PUNCHING TECHNIQUES

Kizami-zuki: the lead jab

Using kizami-zuki *in attack*

The lead jab uses the front hand as a weapon and it is usually directed at the head. As was explained earlier, to ensure that you develop explosiveness, initial training is carried out from a static stance.

To practise the technique, assume *kamae*. Without any unnecessary movement, drive through the rear leg whilst raising the front knee to lift the foot clear of the floor. This allows an unhindered thrust towards the target (Figure 3). Think of the rear leg as a powerful spring tightly

coiled which, when released, provides a tremendous, explosive force. This movement produces a lunging action that is comparable to the fencer's thrust and, as in that art, the lunge is an action of the legs and not the upper body.

Both arms are maintained in the *kamae* position until the very last instant, allowing the legs to do their work first. This both speeds the final delivery and avoids telegraphing the technique. You must aim

FIGURE 3: *Kizami-zuki,* the lead jab.

to coincide your punch with your step: as your front foot strikes the floor, your punch is executed. The action of the arms should be extremely rapid, since they are employed very late in the process. A useful maxim for this example could be: 'punch late and fast, rather than early and slow'.

Now practise the technique from a mobile stance. Continuously change your position relative to your partner, constantly shifting your weight forward and back. As your weight moves over your rear leg begin your attack by allowing that knee to bend and then drive off forcefully by pushing hard into the floor. Make sure that you land on balance, using a firm stance as a basis for your attack.

Some points to avoid are as follows:

1. Do not telegraph your intention, for example by pulling back the elbow prior to punching.

2. Do not lean the upper body forward on execution of the punch, exposing the face to counter-attack.

3. Do not delay the snap back to *kamae*.

4. Do not start the attack from too far away; this results in a failure to reach the target.

As a general principle with all techniques described in this book, practise on your own at first to get the 'feel' of the technique and then try it with a partner, using them as a static target to test your accuracy and distancing. Once you are comfortable with this, increase the challenge by having your partner move to constantly change the distance, and also using light blocks to defend the target.

Finally, work at full speed with your partner trying to block your attacks and immediately counter-attack.

Beware of falling into the trap of launching half-hearted attacks at any time, but particularly when the sparring is pre-arranged. Pair-work should never be regarded as being for the benefit of just one or other of the participants, as if one were 'active' and the other 'passive'. Both karateka should be 'active' and fully involved whether they are attacking or defending. Use this opportunity to try to press home really strong and determined attacks. Provided that your attacks are realistic, your partner should at this stage feel under considerable pressure. Not only will your attacks be sharpened through this practice, but also your partner's defence will be tightened.

When attacking to the face attempt to focus your punch at skin level with the punching arm slightly bent on delivery to ensure that you are able to practise correct distancing. In *kihon*, the distance between the combatants is greater so that a punch or kick can be fully extended to complete the technique, allowing the student to learn their reach with each technique. But the correct distance required for actual fighting is less because, in application, a technique must strike *through* the target to be effective. By using the techniques at a closer range in free-style, the fighting distance will become realistic and as a matter of safety you will need to exercise good control in order that full power can be used. This requires the technique to be 'pulled', snapped back just short of full extension. A karateka who is able to demonstrate good control and at the same time deliver fully focused, powerful techniques has acquired a valuable skill and is a pleasure to watch. Unfortunately, there are some competitors who have very little understanding of control, preferring to allow their techniques literally to bounce off the opponent's body, rather than snapping back to *kamae*. The subject of control in relationship to distance will be discussed further in Chapter 8, under the heading 'Distancing'.

Using kizami-zuki in defence

Kizami-zuki can be a very decisive counterattack. It is especially effective when launched in the nick of time, owing to its simplicity and directness. This method of countering does not require that you block your opponent's attack. Have your partner attack in two ways, using *oi-zuki* (stepping punch) and *ashi-barai* (foot sweep). Both these techniques are described in detail elsewhere in this chapter.

The secret of success in using *kizami-zuki* to nullify an attack is being courageous and applying your punch at the instant your partner attacks. Do not allow them to reach you: close the distance by thrusting forward, spoiling their distance and timing. Immediately they begin their *oi-zuki* attack, thrust through your rear leg and drive directly at your partner. The nature of their attack dictates that they will have to cover a comparatively large distance before they can use their technique. Your forward thrust will enable you to meet them halfway and deliver your punch first.

To demonstrate this point, and as a training exercise, have your partner attack by two counts. At the first count they should step towards you, stopping just short of delivering their punch or focusing their stance, rather like a video freeze-frame. Now make your punch (Figure 5). With their movement arrested, it will be easier for you to gauge the distance and punch with accuracy. Snap back to *kamae*

and thrust away diagonally to the right and rear, to avoid your partner's subsequent lunge. Pay attention to achieving good timing, so that your punch arrives on target at precisely the moment your partner stops. At the second count, as if the video has restarted, your partner should complete their step and deliver their punch, which will of course miss you.

Once you can perform this technique with correct timing and accuracy by two counts, instruct your partner to attack by one count. Split-second timing is required to ensure that you are able to deliver a strong, fully focused punch whilst not placing your partner in any danger. To make the practice as realistic as possible, your partner should concentrate on making a big rapid step, rather than anticipating your counter and pausing mid-step. Also be sure that the practice does not become competitive, with your partner making a shorter step in an attempt to get their punch in, or throwing it in advance of their step. This would not only defeat the object of the exercise, but also be very dangerous.

Now try *kizami-zuki* against your partner's *ashi-barai*, from the *kamae* shown in Figure 4. As the partner begins their foot sweep, with their rear leg, instantly drive in with your punch (Figure 6). Their distance is spoilt by your forward thrust and their foot will miss your ankle. Develop this skill step by step in the same way as was described above for *kizami-zuki*.

Remember to practise both of these routines from a static stance and then practise your anticipation and timing by adding full mobility. Do not worry if you find that you are sometimes 'triggered' into reacting unnecessarily when practising from a mobile stance. At this stage you are

FIGURE 4: The opponents in *kamae* prior to the movements shown in the following figures.

FIGURE 5: This shows *kizami-zuki* being used to counter an opponent's *oi-zuki* attempt. The defender's forward thrust spoils the attacker's distance.

FIGURE 6: *Ashi-barai* is neutralized, the attacker's foot missing the ankle by the defender thrusting forward with *kizami-zuki*.

likely to react to any movement perceived as a threat. Of course, when training from a static position you should move only with your partner's attack. To be 'triggered' prematurely would imply that your partner is telegraphing. It is important that you do move explosively when the attack actually comes; do not be caught 'flat-footed'. With practice and experience you will become more skilful at reacting appropriately. Start lightly and then increase both speed and power.

Gyaku-zuki: the reverse punch

Using gyaku-zuki in attack

Students will recognize that the reverse punch is the standard, most often employed, counter-attack in basic one-step sparring and semi-free-style sparring. It has the benefit of being the most practised and therefore the most familiar technique and is also a major scoring technique in competition.

The *gyaku-zuki* is delivered with the rear hand, the target being either the head or body (Figure 7). Practise the punch in drill form from a static *kamae*. The benefit of *hikete* can really be appreciated with this particular technique. Concentrate on rapidly pulling back the lead hand as you punch to feel an increase in the power of the punch. Reach can be achieved by lowering the stance and driving the hip on the same side as the punch, as far forward as possible. Achieving this extra reach can be particularly important when attacking as the opponent will often attempt to move away at the last instant but might underestimate the distance you can cover. The

footwork used is very similar to that used for *kizami-zuki*, in that a forceful thrust through the rear leg initiates the attack.

Now practise the technique whilst moving in *kamae*. It is useful to sometimes have someone to call out the command to attack, providing you with a stimulus to react to, so that your reactions can be improved. Remember to use the rear leg, fully engage the hip and deliver the punch from a strong stance.

The points to avoid are the same as for *kizami-zuki*, plus the following:

1. Do not forget to use the hips fully, otherwise the punch will lack both reach and power. The stance employed should be slightly wider than that for *kizami-zuki* to ensure that the hip on the punching side can be driven fully forward.

2. Do not lean the upper body forward; this interferes with the hip action.

FIGURE 7: *Gyaku-zuki,* the reverse punch.

Acquire a sense of distance by pairing up and attacking first from a fixed distance, and then add footwork to practise the punch from different ranges, with your partner blocking lightly. As before, complete the exercise by making spirited attacks which your partner should try to block and immediately counter.

Using gyaku-zuki in defence

Practise defending against your partner's *kizami-zuki*. As they thrust at you, sway your upper body back, moving your face directly away from the attack. At the same time, take your rear foot backwards a few inches but do not shift your front foot. This fixes the distance for your counter, making it unnecessary for you to gain ground. From the starting position shown in Figure 4, move your weight over your rear leg as you block with your lead arm using a sweeping palm block, *nagashi-uke* (Figure 8). Make sure that your block deflects their punch to your right side, but not in a pressing action as in a palm-heel block. You should try instead to redirect the punch in a flowing action past the right side of your head, drawing your partner onto your counter, rather than just pushing their arm away.

As their punch is completed, drive forward through your rear leg and immediately hit back with your *gyaku-zuki* to your partner's midsection (Figure 9). The feeling is as though you catch them before they have been able to snap back to *kamae*. Follow the training principles detailed previously to build up the practice. You can begin as before by using two counts. The first count has your partner stopping their punch whilst you practise your block and rear leg action. The second count can be used to try to beat your partner's return to *kamae* by quickly delivering your punch.

FIGURE 8: This and Figure 9 show *gyaku-zuki* used in defence, the partner's *kizama-zuki* first being blocked by means of a palm block.

FIGURE 9: Once the *kizami-zuki* has been blocked (Figure 8), the *gyaku-zuki* finds the partner's midsection.

Oi-zuki: the lunge punch

Using oi-zuki *in attack*

When used in attack, *oi-zuki* requires a punch to be delivered at the completion of a striding step (Figure 10). Caution should be exercised as the distance covered with this attack gives your opponent plenty of time to react, robbing it of any chance of scoring if you are inept enough to telegraph your intention.

This technique is also called the 'stepping punch' and the weapon used is the hand on the same side as the advancing foot. To practise the punch, assume left foot forward *kamae*. Simultaneously pull through your front leg and push through your rear leg to achieve speed in your step. Note that this differs from the lower, basic stance, *zenkutsu-*

dachi (front stance), in which a pushing action of the rear leg is not normally emphasized. This is because in the basic stance the rear leg is fully locked out and

FIGURE 10: Using *oi-zuku,* the lunge punch, in attack.

the weight is predominantly over the front foot, which favours a pulling action through that leg as opposed to any rear leg push.

The last part of the movement, with the right leg passing close to the left, is similar to the basic form. The left leg now drives the whole body forward. Extra reach can be achieved by landing the foot on a direct line with the rear foot and twisting the torso so that the chest faces the side rather than the front as in the basic form. The resulting punch is able to impart a considerable shock to the target. Practise hand-foot co-ordination by timing your punch as your right foot strikes the floor. Stop forward momentum by using your front leg like a buttress against your body. The feeling is that you stamp into the floor and strongly tense that leg to apply the brakes. Simultaneous tensing of all the muscles at this point helps to activate *kime*, focusing and releasing all your power through the knuckles of your fore-fist.

The experienced competitor sees the lunge punch as a valuable asset to their armoury. If used decisively, it is extremely piercing and powerful. Sensei Yahara, who was one of the fiercest fighters of the Japan Karate Association, once stated that he favoured *oi-zuki* above all other techniques, finding most success with it when he was forced to defend himself in real-life situations! With subtle changes in timing, i.e. punching just prior to, or just after the step, the punch can be irritatingly difficult to block. This is undoubtedly due to the fact that so many thousands of hours and repetitions have been devoted to timing *age-uke* (rising-block), not so much to the punch itself, but to the opponent's step.

In basic five-step and one-step sparring we are taught to step and punch

simultaneously when using *oi-zuki*. That is the general rule. It is therefore natural to time the basic block with the partner's step. If your immediate reaction is to disagree with this, then I would suggest that you might like to try five-step sparring with a beginner who has yet to achieve hand-foot co-ordination. The results can sometimes be interesting! This rule can be somewhat relaxed when it comes to a *kumite* match. Further advice on using timing to confuse your opponent will be highlighted in the next chapter and it can be applied very effectively to this technique.

Practise *oi-zuki* following the method I have described. That is, begin by working with the technique on your own and then progress to the partner work. Since it is intrinsically an attack, it is difficult to employ the lunge punch as a defensive measure without changing its fundamental nature, so no defensive strategies are suggested here.

The points to avoid are as for previous punches, plus the following:

1 Do not lift, turn out or pull back the front (left) foot prior to stepping with the right foot. This is a common error which serves to telegraph the technique or, in the case of pulling back the front foot, to impair reach.

Uraken-uchi: the back-fist strike

Using uraken *in attack*

Apart from the *tettsui-uchi* (bottom-fist strike), which is seldom used, the back-fist is the only hand technique not employing the *seiken* (fore-fist) allowed in competition. Strikes involving the open hand directed towards vulnerable targets, such as

FIGURE 11: *Uraken-uchi*, the back-fist strike.

the eyes, are forbidden. The back-fist strike is a very useful tool, often best employed as a counter-attack, when it is difficult to block. The urge to use it at every opportunity must be resisted, as it is often perceived to lack power. Weaker competitors will use it in a 'flicky' fashion which serves more as an irritation to the opponent than a threat. Used correctly it can turn the tide of a match in your favour.

The weapon in this case is the back of the closed fist (Figure 11) and the target is usually the face and neck. When the technique is used in its fullest form, the shoulder acts as a fulcrum with the elbow drawing the fist from a starting-point on the far side of the body anywhere on a vertical line from the neck down to the hip. The attack is then delivered to the target in an arcing action. If the starting point is the hip, then the movement should resemble the drawing and cutting action of a sword. Many

of the *kata* employ *uraken* in precisely this way. On completion, the fist is sharply snapped back to the nearside chest. Unlike the punching techniques, *uraken* requires a preparation which moves the hand away from the *kamae* position, which can telegraph your intention. For this reason it is important to strike economically, dispensing with the obvious preparation used in basics. Using the same footwork as in delivering *kizami-zuki*, quickly pull your lead fist back towards the far side of your body and, by leading with your elbow, draw the fist out to the target and sharply snap it back to your chest in a whipping action. The technique is frequently used in an abbreviated form in *kumite* as an opportunist counter-attack, rather like the example in the *kata heian sandan*, with the shoulder being more or less fixed and the elbow acting as a pivot.

The following are points to avoid:

1. Do not use too much tension in the arm; this will slow the action.

2. Do not over-extend the elbow on delivery of the technique; this can badly injure the joint.

3. Do not 'freeze' in the finished position, with your elbow up; this leaves you in a vulnerable position.

Using uraken *in defence*

Have your partner attack with *chudan* (middle-level) *mawashi-geri*. Your defence consists in moving the target area out of reach of their foot, parrying your partner's kick and spinning them around, thus

FIGURE 12: The first stage in using *uraken* to counter *mawashi-geri*, the round-house kick. The right hand ensures that the opponent's kick continues in its natural course.

FIGURE 13: Continuation of the action shown in Figure 12.

placing yourself in an advantageous position from which to deliver your back-fist.

As your partner kicks, withdraw your front foot, moving your torso back and beyond the reach of their low round-house kick. Use your right hand to ensure that the kick continues in its natural course (Figure 12). To gain a clearer impression of this method, imagine that you start a child's merry-go-round by pushing it. As it picks up speed, you reach and catch each hand-rail, pulling it in turn towards you and releasing it as it passes you. With each successive pull the ride is easier to move as it builds up momentum. The action of catching your partner's ankle, pulling their leg past your right side and spinning them around (Figure 13) works in the same way as assisting the child's ride. You simply have to time your catch so that it assists the momentum of the leg and prevents your partner from recovering. If you time it accurately you will find that your partner will be spun completely around so that they land with their back towards you.

The escape begins by pulling back your front foot so that it comes close to your rear one. You continue by thrusting it diagonally to your left side without pausing, co-ordinated with your sweeping arm action. This will place you in a good position to counter, even if you were unable to spin your partner around completely, so as to be behind them. From this position, without delay, you should deliver your right *uraken* to your partner's head, thrusting forward to gain ground if necessary (Figure 14).

Practice method for training in all the above hand techniques in drill form

As an addition to training in the above techniques, you will gain benefit from practising them all as a combination on your own. Starting from *kamae*, drive into *kizami-zuki*, immediately snapping back. Perform the remainder of the above hand techniques one by one until you have completed them all, each time snapping sharply back to *kamae*. This kind of practice is valuable for 'grooving' the various techniques into your subconscious, and provides a method for evaluating not only the differences between them, but also their relationship to one another, allowing for direct comparison of their unique qualities. The routine is illustrated in Figure 15.

FIGURE 14: Once the opponent has been spun around, an *uraken* can be delivered to the partner's head.

FIGURE 15: Method for practising the various hand techniques. The numbers show the order in which the techniques are performed. Step forward to execute No 4 and step back to right *kame*. Thrust forward to execute No 5 and snap back.

KICKING TECHNIQUES

Mae-geri: **the front kick**

Using mae-geri *in attack*

With sufficient training, *mae-geri* (Figure 16) can be the most direct and effective of the leg techniques. However, most students make the mistake of attacking from too great a distance with the result either that the toes can be damaged by the opponent's block or that the kick will simply fail to reach the target. Used at the correct distance, it is a very rapid kick, employing the power of both hips, and can be delivered with either a snapping or thrusting action.

As was explained in the previous chapter, there must be no indication given as to the type of kick you intend to deliver. Start by lifting your rear foot clear off the floor – not by raising the heel as you would do when walking, but by bending the knee and keeping the ankle strongly flexed so as to ensure that the entire sole is raised. Continue lifting the knee to the front with the leg fully bent. As the knee reaches approximately waist height, start to extend the leg towards the target and at the last moment engage the hips by thrusting them forcefully to the front. The striking area is usually the ball of the foot, but the entire sole or even the heel can be used for the thrust or snap kick. After rapidly and completely withdrawing the kicking foot you can exploit the momentum generated by the initial thrust by immediately stepping forward into a balanced and strong position. If the action of 'freezing' your elbow in position after making *uraken-uchi* makes you vulnerable to counter-attack, then certainly the act of kicking and pausing with the knee up can

FIGURE 16: *Mae-geri,* the front kick.

also leave you in a vulnerable position. Provided that a second kick is intended, before the opponent can recover, or *zanshin* is maintained, then this is acceptable. However, when it is your intention to use only *mae-geri,* you should try to pick up your leg, use it and step forward in the same time that it takes to perform *oi-zuki*.

With a snap kick there is no noticeable pause at the moment that the leg is fully extended. Like snap punches in which the hands are immediately returned to *kamae,* the leg also is quickly brought back to the knee-up position. In the thrust version, the leg is momentarily locked out and the effectiveness of the kick relies mostly on the action of the hips. In the snap kick, it is the rapid action of straightening and then bending of the knee that imparts the shock. When thrusting a kick, any kick, think of your thrust as being a fast push. A snap kick should have a piercing, penetrative quality whilst a thrust kick should be forceful enough to bodily propel an opponent away from you.

Apart from kicking from the incorrect distance, another mistake made with the front kick is the tendency to allow the foot to travel upwards in an arc. This is particularly true of the snap kick. If this happens, the kick has little effect. To avoid this, kick no higher than the stomach and be sure to drive the hips *forward* into the target. The foot should actually travel on a straight line from the floor to the target and not in an arc, as some people imagine.

Practise the kick in drill form by breaking it down into its component parts, pausing in each position: (a) lift the knee; (b) extend your kick and hold; (c) return to knee-up position; (d) step forwards or back.

Now practise the kick against your partner's abdomen. Have them stand in *fudo-dachi*, but ask that they keep their hips square to the front to provide a good target. Start by training your kick according to the 'step-by-step' principle, each time ensuring that the kick makes some, though not excessive, contact with your partner's stomach, which should be tensed. Observe for tell-tale signs of poor form, such as your foot skimming upwards instead of striking cleanly, directed horizontally straight into the target. Then practise with full speed and power, exercising good control. Build up to full mobility and have your partner try to escape and parry the kick. Finally, they can block and then counter-attack using *gyaku-zuki*.

The following are points to avoid:

1. Do not telegraph the kick by, for example, moving the front, support-ing foot in any way, or leaning the upper body forward prior to the kick.

2. Do not drop the guard during the kick.

3. Do not swing the foot upwards when kicking.

4. Do not lean the upper body forward as the kick is applied.

Using mae-geri *in defence*

Train on this defensive application of the kick by using timing in much the same way as you practised your defensive *kizami-zuki*. Have your partner attack using *oi-zuki*. In the instant that they begin to step, use your rear leg to catch them before they reach you (Figure 17). This example enables you to appreciate fully the reach advantage the leg has over the arm. If you catch them early enough you will be able to thrust-kick them and stop them in their tracks, whilst you are able to continue your movement so that your right leg is forward upon landing. Should your kick be a fraction later it is wiser to use a snap kick and immediately step back so that you remain in left *kamae*. If you attempt a thrust kick when your partner is almost upon you, there is the risk that you may be bowled over backwards by their momentum, which would, of course, render your kick ineffective. Timing is the key.

Practise the technique by one action, but instruct your partner to 'freeze' their step midway to enable you to time your kick properly, placing your thrust kick against their abdomen, which should be tensed. An explosive start is their priority and you will use this as a trigger for your kick.

When practising the same response,

FIGURE 17: *Mae-geri* in·defence, used here to counter *oi-zuki*.

but using a snapping action with your kick instead of a thrust, you can ask your partner to perform the entire movement, culminating with their punch. Now you must use your foot as you did your hand in any of the defensive hand techniques described earlier. That is, you should try to develop fine control with your counter, withdrawing the foot the instant it touches their body, not just allowing your foot to bounce off. As soon as you withdraw the foot, step back to your initial stance. You should strive for the kind of control that does not inhibit your partner's step in any way. They should not feel uneasy about making their attack for fear of an uncontrolled kick, so they can attack you with vigour and full confidence which will give you a realistic assessment of your speed and accuracy. Practising in this way also gives your partner the opportunity to improve their *oi-zuki*, timing their punch so that it is focused close to your chin as your foot is returned to the floor. Remember to build up the routine in the same way as before, by starting from static positions and then adding full mobility.

Yoko-geri: the side kick

Using yoko-geri *in attack*

The side kick (Figure 18) is taught in two distinct forms in basics: as a thrust kick, where the hips are strongly applied and the foot travels in essentially a straight line; and as a snap kick, where the hips are not engaged and the foot travels up in an arc. In a self-defence situation the snap kick would be devastating as a blow under the jaw but the difficulty of control and the need for a clear route up in front of the opponent's chest to the jaw means that it cannot readily be applied to a *jodan* (head) target in competition sparring, so

FIGURE 18: *Yoko-geri*, the side kick.

twist the hips through 90 degrees, pivoting outwards on the ball of the supporting foot so that the toes point in almost the opposite direction to the intended kick. Your weight should settle on the heel of the supporting foot, with the leg strongly tensed and the knee slightly bent to absorb the shock of impact. The kicking leg is extended in a straight line and the hips simultaneously driven forcefully in the direction of the target. The striking area of the foot is either the edge of the foot or the heel. The leg is quickly withdrawn at the end of the kick, to enable a speedy return to stance.

Practise the form of this kick in basics by breaking it down into several components: (a) raise the knee; (b) pivot, kick and lock the leg right out, holding the position; (c) withdraw the leg, pivoting back so that you face the front; (d) step back or forward.

Check that, as you pivot, your kicking foot is not caused to describe an arc, as you would expect if you were performing the round-house kick. Now practise the

only the thrust kick is considered here. It is best used against the body.

Yoko-geri kekomi, using the rear leg from *fudo-dachi*, is, however, difficult to apply with any sharpness in competition. It often has the appearance of being dull or mistimed and ends up resembling an awkward push. With correct timing, however, it can be a decisive technique. For a more powerful thrust, it is possible to attack using the forward leg after shifting the rear foot forward to gain momentum and distance. For the purposes of this text the rear leg only will be used. Kicking techniques using the front leg will be described in detail in Volume 2.

Begin the thrust kick by lifting the rear knee to the front as if you were going to make *mae-geri*. In a continuous action,

kick by putting all the components together and making two smooth, flowing actions. The first action involves raising the knee, pivoting and thrusting the leg out straight, with the second action smoothly withdrawing the leg by bending the knee and then returning to stance. The resulting kick should conform to the principles you have developed in the 'step-by-step' technique. By adding motion, you bring additional forces into play, some of which will help your kick and others which will hinder it. For example, in the 'step-by-step' version, you will find it difficult to pivot and kick smoothly from the knee-up position. You will want to drop your knee a little and then spring or bounce into your kick. Performing the kick as a whole, you will have no such problem as the initial impetus gained by lifting the foot quickly from the floor will ensure that the pivot is made easy. Whilst this makes this particular movement a little easier, the drawback is that the pivoting action conspires to change the nature of the kick from a straight line to one which is curved, as it is precisely this type of hip action that favours the round-house kick.

You can compensate for this to a large extent by working on converting your pivoting action into a pushing or thrusting action. At the completion of your pivot, smoothly thrust both hips towards the target. This will help to counter the initial twisting action. Your thrust should compel you to step forward because your centre of gravity will take your weight in the direction of your kick. Do not try to duplicate the position you were able to maintain in the 'step-by-step' routine, where you were balanced statically on one leg with your kicking leg locked out. If you were to try to emulate this position in reality, you would be catapulted backwards on impact, being unable to absorb the shock reaction of your kick. Neither should you try to balance on your support leg, having withdrawn your kicking leg – that was just an exercise. Now you must step down immediately.

Build up the practice of yoko-geri for attack in precisely the same way as you did for mae-geri, by working on the kick in drill form and then developing it using a partner. Concentrate on not completely locking the leg out as you kick them. Exercise the same sort of control as you would with a punch, and as you connect, rapidly withdraw the foot off the target. The following are points to avoid:

1. Do not telegraph the kick in any way, by for example dropping the guard, moving the front foot, etc., prior to kicking.

2. Do not twist the upper body away as the knee comes up.

3. Do not swing the foot in an arc.

4. Do not try to maintain balance on one leg, push all your weight at the target.

Using yoko-geri in defence

Your partner will attack using *kizami-zuki* (Figure 19). As they thrust forward, shift your front foot to the left side and at the same time block their punch using your right hand (Figure 20). Raise your right knee and immediately kick *yoko-geri* to their midsection (Figures 21 and 22). Practise the move by the count. On the first count they attack and you side-step, blocking the punch. On the second count raise your knee and on the third count kick. Continue with the fourth count by withdrawing and stepping down. When you feel confident with this, do it by two counts: start in the same way but combine counts 2, 3 and 4 to perform the whole kick. Check that your distance is correct for your kick. You should be close enough to connect with the kick without having to overstretch. If you are able to lock your leg out fully, then you are too far away. Remember: distance should be realistic. Now practise by one count and concentrate on closing the gap between your step, block and counter-kick. There should be no discernible pause following your block. Your response must be immediate. Although the idea is impossible in real terms, think of the concept of 'simultaneous reaction'.

Develop the routine as before, building

FIGURE 19: This and Figures 20–22 show *yoko-geri* used to counter *kizami-zuku*, the lead jab. Here the opponent starts to attack.

FIGURE 20: Blocking the punch and sidestepping.

FIGURE 21: The knee is raised in preparation for *yoko-geri*.

FIGURE 22: Completion of *yoko-geri.*

in speed and power and adding mobility.

Mawashi-geri: the round-house kick

Using mawashi-geri *in attack*

Sometimes called 'the competition kick', the *mawashi-geri* (Figure 23) is nevertheless a very effective weapon both on or off the mats. It is a beautifully versatile kick which feels more natural to perform than the side kick. For competition purposes, the striking area is usually the instep, which provides for a safer kick, the ball of the foot being considered too dangerous a weapon. The target can be the head or anywhere on the torso, particularly the stomach, the sides and lower back.

As described elsewhere in this book, the modern version of this kick is performed with economy and (because of a more direct route) speed in mind, but should still be capable of delivering a very powerful

FIGURE 23: *Mawashi-geri,* the round-house kick.

shock to the target. An ability to deliver rapid techniques with little or no telegraphing is a major factor for success on the mats, a point that has been stressed previously. The preparation required to make the 'traditional' *mawashi-geri* suggests that it would be unwise to use it, on the basis that it can so easily be 'read'.

Practise the kick in drill form: (a) Raise the knee to the front as in *mae-geri*. (b) Then in a pivoting action, similar to the movement required for *yoko-geri*, turn the hips through 90 degrees. (c) Snap the foot out. The resulting arc that your foot travels through is somewhat smaller than the arc described in the 'traditional' kick, but for this reason it will be more difficult to read. (d) Snap the leg back and step forwards or back.

Develop the kick using a partner in the same way as described previously. Initially work on static positions, and then do the complete kick, working on accuracy, speed and reach by projecting your centre of gravity towards the target. With the introduction of mobility, follow the same procedure as previously described; try to 'score' on your partner as they defend. The points to avoid are as follows

1. Do not telegraph the kick in any way. Minimize unnecessary movements.

2. Do not allow the foot to skim upwards when kicking to the head; use the hip to control the kick so that it strikes the target from the side.

3. Do not allow the knee to drop during or after the kick; snap the leg back with the knee still up, and then lower it.

4. Do not lean too far to the side when kicking.

5. Do not allow the heel of the support foot to rise during the kick.

Using mawashi-geri *in defence*

Your partner will attack with *gyaku-zuki*, thrusting forward to cover distance. Respond by withdrawing your front leg and so removing the target from their reach. As an insurance also block downwards in case their reach is extensive (Figure 24). Immediately change sides and kick *mawashi-geri* to

FIGURE 24: Blocking *gyaku-zuki*, in preparation for a counter-attack using *mawashi-geri*.

FIGURE 25: *Mawashi-geri* following the countering of the opponent's *gyaku-zuki* as shown in Figure 24.

their head or side before they can recover (Figure 25).

Practise the technique by the count. At the first count your partner will launch their attack and you will make your escape, blocking down with your lead arm. Your feet should be fairly close together at this point with both knees bent. In stepping back you have achieved two objectives, that of escaping and also that of positioning yourself for your counter-kick. At the second count, your partner returns to *kamae* as you quickly pivot and kick. At this point you can really work on your speed by trying to kick them before they can return to *kamae*.

Next, perform the step, block and kick by one count, ensuring that each time you make only one step, gauging the distance correctly for your kick. Most importantly, do not kick from too close a range, where

your opponent would be able to reach you with their hands.

Ashi-barai: the foot sweep

Using ashi-barai *in attack*

The foot-sweep (Figure 26) can literally be your opponent's downfall. Although it is not a scoring technique in itself, it allows you to follow immediately with a decisive attack. *Ashi-barai* in its simplest form can be used to unsettle an opponent, creating enough distraction to destroy their composure. At its spectacular best, it is called *kuzushi*, 'crushing the enemy', and can completely up-end the opponent, leaving them with no possibility of being able to defend themself. This was a favourite technique of Sensei Enoeda, one he

FIGURE 26: *Ashi-barai*, the foot sweep.

employed to great effect in his competition days. There are several methods, including sweeps that attack one or both of the opponent's legs in a variety of ways, using the instep, sole or calf muscle. The way your opponent has their weight distributed between their feet is an important factor to consider and can mean the difference between the success and failure of the technique.

Being able to use the foot-sweep effectively requires good timing, a sense of your opponent's balance and commitment. Skilled competitors gain an almost instinctive feel for its use, so that the technique looks wonderfully simple. A competitor of recent years who has used this technique with enthusiasm and great style is the London-based fighter Elwyn Hall. He demonstrated his immense skill at the 1990 World Championship, in which

his opponents were lucky if they remained on their feet!

Ashi-barai when applied as an attack can be considered as a kick. Its delivery should be very sharp, but unlike kicks to the head in competition, which are focused for control, it must continue right through the target to have any effect. It is a difficult technique to practise with a partner in a pre-arranged situation, because it works best when they do not expect it. No one likes the feeling of being knocked off their feet and crashing to the floor in an undignified heap. Tell your partner that you intend to practise your foot-sweep and watch their expression alter. An 'over-co-operative' partner, wanting to control their fall, will tend to spoil your practice by making it too easy for you, with the result that you will not really be sweeping them at all. Another response, usually employed by a larger partner, is to 'root' their stance, with no intention of allowing you to make them fall over.

A compromise is necessary in this situation, otherwise repeated unsuccessful attempts can be painful and damaging for both the attacker and the receiver. During practice you must make a determined effort to sweep your partner, otherwise you will never get the 'feel' of the technique, but they are allowed to take 'the sting' out of the technique by moving their foot in the direction of your sweep. This enables them to remain on their feet, but will also allow you to practise commitment, accuracy and follow-through. This provides a degree of realism, but the only way you can really test your foot-sweep is by using it spontaneously in free-sparring.

Develop your attacking *ashi-barai* in the following way. (a) From *kamae*, transfer your weight completely onto your front foot as you begin the sweep with your rear foot. Reach to the front in an arc with the edge of the foot gliding just above the surface so that the sole of the foot is exposed. (b) Take the foot to its maximum reach, maintaining a guarding position with the hands, and at this point lift the foot directly upwards in a scooping action by bending and slightly raising the knee. You should try to get your foot as high as your opposite knee with your shin as horizontal as possible. Step down and forward to stance.

Depending on what type of sweep you intend to make, either fully twist the hips into the sweep, in which case your objective would be to throw your opponent, or keep the hips square and just use the power of the leg to disrupt their balance.

Practise *ashi-barai* with your partner by attacking their forward ankle using the sole of your rear foot. It is essential that you 'set up' your partner in order to make the sweep work. Do this by moving to your right side until their feet appear on a single line. From this position, which is the optimum position to apply your sweep, their front foot will obscure the rear foot. Provided that they do not adjust their foot position, their stance will now appear very narrow and consequently their balance will become precarious and susceptible to your sweep. In reality, an opponent in this situation would almost certainly realize their predicament and shift their feet to return to a more balanced and secure position. However, for the sake of development, it is necessary to suspend reality momentarily to gain any benefit from this exercise.

Attack their nearest ankle using *ashi-barai* following the method described above. Aim through the ankle so that there is a large 'follow-through' movement.

If you stop as you connect, your sweep will have little effect. Your partner should shift their weight back a little so that they can lift their front foot and 'ride' your sweep. You will probably not be able to throw them, but if you connect with good timing you will still be able to disturb their balance.

Continue making attacks with *ashi-barai* and then introduce punches: *oi-zuki* to the back of your partner's head as they spin, or *gyaku-zuki* before they can recover, but continue to concentrate on your sweeping action. Ensure that you attack with explosiveness, trying to catch them before they can transfer their weight. The feeling is that you intend to actually throw them. It is their responsibility to move quickly enough to prevent this. The points to avoid are as follows:

1. Do not lift the sweeping foot until the target (ankle) is struck. If you sweep too high, the technique will be ineffective and could damage your opponent's knee.

2. Do not sweep using the inside edge of the foot; the sole should be used.

3. Do not sweep in such a way that if you miss, you throw yourself! The technique should be controlled throughout. Be ready to follow up instantly.

Using ashi-barai *in defence*

Your partner will have no choice but to fall in this application, provided that they fully commit their attack. It is therefore courteous to advise them that they will fall in order that they can prepare for the eventuality. This defensive *ashi-barai* relies on split-second timing and requires courage but is very effective, giving the attacker the almost authentic sensation of having slipped on a banana skin!

From *kamae*, instruct your partner to attack with a committed, forceful *oi-zuki*. As they begin their attack, shift your weight entirely onto your rear foot, keeping your guard. Just as they are about to land and deliver their punch, sweep their advancing foot (Figure 27). If you time it to perfection, you should have no problem in throwing your partner (Figure 28). If you mistime it, especially leaving it too late, they will be able to lock their stance, making the sweep very difficult to apply, when it should be effortless. Worse still, they may be able to catch you with their punch. Remember to follow up with a punch or stamp immediately that they are felled, otherwise they may be able to roll away or lash out at you from the floor.

To score in competition, it is essential that your follow-up is immediate. If you hesitate the point will not be given.

Practice method for training in all the above kicks in drill form

As with the punching techniques, it is a good idea to practise kicks in a consecutive way so as to 'groove' the techniques into the subconscious. By training in this way you are constantly reinforcing patterns of movement and programming the muscles so that they 'remember' how to move for each individual kick.

Practise the routine illustrated in Figure 29. Perform each kick slowly, using the 'step-by-step' method, holding each position for a few seconds to develop strength and awareness of the technique, then step back to stance. Practise each kick in succession in this way, using the 'knee-up'

FIGURE 27: *Ashi-barai* used to counter *oi-zuku*. If carefully timed, the opponent will be felled.

position as the common starting and finishing point for all the kicks save for the *ashi-barai*. With the execution of the foot sweep, which can also be held out on completion, step forward and then begin the whole sequence again, having changed legs. Another useful method for developing strength and explosiveness is by moving quickly from one static position to the next. When doing this, do not allow the leg to drop on completing a kick; try to maintain *kime* until you snap the leg back. Next, practise each kick by one action, working on a smooth delivery and paying particular attention to the start of each kick, which, apart from the *ashi-barai*, should be identical. Then kick as fast as possible and try not to allow the form to deteriorate.

Finally, increase the challenge by building the kicks up in sequence from the knee-up position, again using the 'step-by-step' sequence. You can vary the practice as before, by either moving slowly from one position to the next or moving explosively. This method precludes the inclusion of *ashi-barai* as its completed position does not complement the other kicks in this exercise. Begin by raising the knee with the hips square to the front. This is the starting and finishing position for the three kicks. Now perform *mae-geri* and hold the kick extended for a few seconds. Pull back and, without dropping the knee, pivot and kick *yoko-geri*, locking the leg out and holding. Withdraw and again, without dropping the knee, kick *mawashi-geri*, hold and return to the 'knee-up' position. Finally return to stance. Repeat this routine several times until you feel fatigued and then change legs and repeat. If you have any energy left you can then perform each kick in fast succession from the 'knee-up' position, stepping back only after having completed all the kicks.

FIGURE 28: A successful *ashi-barai*.

FIGURE 29: Practice method for training in the
various kicks. The numbers show the order
in which the movements are executed.

2.

3.

4.

1.

5.

8 MAKING TECHNIQUES WORK FOR YOU: THE STRATEGY

This chapter will describe additional skills and the tactics which you will need to add to your armoury of techniques before you compete.

DISTANCING

Distancing is referred to in Japanese as *ma-ai*. Simply speaking, it is the distance you maintain from your opponent which would force them to make a committed lunge in order to reach you. At the same time the distance must not be so great as to deny yourself the opportunity for attack. Maintaining this delicate balance is a crucial factor in fighting.

Distancing is also the constant that governs the success or failure of *timing*. In order to benefit from good timing, you also have to be in the right place. The gap between yourself and your opponent determines whether you should select long- or close-range techniques, and different distances are required for snapping or thrusting techniques.

In a more subtle way, distance is altered by 'moving within the stance'. This is achieved, without moving the feet, by shifting the centre of gravity, as would be

the case when changing from front to back stance or the reverse.

Correct distancing in fighting is more complex than appears at first glance and, not surprisingly, it causes many students difficulties. During grading examinations, students frequently perform basic *kumite* with little or no appreciation of correct distance. At worst this can result in injury. At best it gives the appearance that the participants are divided by an invisible wall! Poor control in free fighting is usually attributable to an inability to 'arrest' or stop a technique on the target, whilst in basic sparring excessive contact can only be due to faulty distancing.

Control is continually stressed in the karate dojo, but is not usually related to distancing. In sports where contact is permissible, or even mandatory, such as boxing, distancing is a more tangible element because an error of judgement means an instant and painful lesson! In contrast, the emphasis in karate is placed on the ability to stop or 'arrest' a technique on or just short of the target. Any physical movement or 'pattern' that is repeated often enough will be automatically programmed into the subconscious so that it becomes a conditioned reflex, so we must

Ronnie jumps and kicks *ura-mawashi-geri* to the head of his 208cm (6ft 8in) opponent, Leslie Jensen, in the semi-finals of the World Championship, Sunderland 1990.

be careful not to train ourselves to fight at the wrong distance.

When practising *kihon* (basics), the element of distancing is not emphasized. This is added with the introduction of partner work and formal *yakusoku gohon kumite*, pre-arranged five-step sparring, which uses the same techniques as those learned in *kihon*. This type of practice requires the participants to stand a little further away from each other than would actually be effective in real combat. Counter-attacks using the arms employ a thrusting action where techniques are fully locked out and held on the target for a few seconds. For example, when executing *gyaku-zuki*, the punching arm

should be held straight with the fore-fist just touching the target. It is unnecessary to stop or 'pull' techniques short of the target because the distance between defender and attacker is based on the length of the defender's arm. This provides an effective and precise method of measuring correct distance when applying *basic* technique to *kumite*, and enables the student to fully extend each technique in the same way as in *kihon*.

We can conclude, therefore, that the most useful skill developed in formal, basic sparring is not the understanding of distance, but the awareness of *reach*. Through this type of sparring you will learn to gauge distance accurately, using

FIGURE 30: A non-scoring punch. The arm is fully extended but has failed to reach its target.

FIGURE 31: Another non-scoring punch. It has not been adequately controlled and would almost certainly warrant disqualification.

the simple measurement of the length of your extended arm or, if kicking, the length of the leg. You will also learn to use your hips, stance and body rotation to increase reach and learn the exact distance you need to fully extend your technique.

Difficulties can arise when you try to apply the distancing learned in basic sparring to *jyu-kumite*, free-style sparring, which is the form of fighting developed for competitions. Many people do not understand the reason behind the use of snapping techniques. They are not just a different style of delivery, but are actually required by the nature of this form of sparring, because to leave the arm

FIGURE 32: The essence of control. The bent arm indicates an ability to stop the punch accurately on the target.

extended would allow the arm or sleeve to be grabbed, and not snapping back leaves the target undefended. To make the practice of free-style safer, techniques are snapped back at the instant of contact, just short of full extension. The idea is that the technique *could* be completed but you *choose* to pull it back, demonstrating both mental and physical control. Because you are at the true distance for actual combat and the technique is not fully extended at the moment of contact, you need to be closer than in basic sparring. It can now be seen how control and correct fighting distance are related.

Illustrated here are three punching attacks which on first examination may look very similar. In fact, only one of them should score in competition. Ronnie's attack shown in Figure 30 should not score because even though his arm is fully extended, the target has not been reached. His attack in Figure 31 should certainly not score. It demonstrates a punch which has not been controlled, but which has been thrust right through the target, probably causing severe injury to the opponent. Such a lack of control would almost certainly justify disqualification. The final illustration (Figure 32) demonstrates the essential hallmarks of good control. Ronnie shows great skill in focusing his punch right on his opponent's chin, at skin level. The punching arm is slightly bent, which indicates his ability to stop his technique accurately on the target.

Perhaps there is an argument for the introduction of some appropriate skills into the *Kyu* grading syllabus, which at present does not require 6th, 5th and 4th *Kyus* to demonstrate free-style methods, presumably because such techniques are considered to be 'advanced'. This situation allows a green belt to enter competitions legitimately but with no verification that they have undergone the correct training and preparation to ensure their own safety and that of their opponent. The attitude that people with some knowledge of basic karate, but lacking essential skills, will benefit from 'having a go' is potentially dangerous and certainly irresponsible.

TIMING

Most of the drills in this book involve the use of good timing. Having this ability implies that a fighter must also be prepared, and in a state of *zanshin*. This allows a fighter to be poised on a 'hair trigger' to dispose quickly of an opponent who makes an *anticipated* movement. Learn to anticipate correctly and your timing will assume an almost magical quality. But anticipate incorrectly at your peril! Great care should be taken not to succumb to an opponent's false movements, which are usually designed to induce you to act recklessly. A fighter who is not particularly fast but who has a good sense of timing can make up for their lack of speed by simply moving at their opponent at the right time. In fact, their speed will appear to increase dramatically, being combined with the attacker's momentum in much the same way as a vehicle travelling in the opposite direction to the one in which you are travelling appears suddenly to accelerate as it passes your car. As with distance, timing cannot be improved by practising *kihon* or *kata*. The best way to develop timing is to constantly work on *kumite* drills that pit you directly against your partner.

You can continue to practise the methods described in the previous chapter to improve timing: for example, negating your partner's attack by thrusting towards them and spoiling their distance in the way described. This strategy requires excellent timing in order to be successful. Just as it is best to gauge the effectiveness of *ashi-barai* by using it without pre-warning your partner, it is wise to practise occasionally using timing during unrehearsed sparring. As with any technique that you wish to test under 'realistic' circumstances, it is preferable to use it sparingly, otherwise your partner will learn to expect it and may frustrate your attempts.

Practise also using timing when attacking with *oi-zuki*. Frustrate your opponent's attempts to block by deliberately mistiming your step and punch. Break the basic rule of punching simultaneously with your step and instead throw your punch a little early or a little late. Your opponent will probably wrongly anticipate the delivery of your attack with the moment you focus your stance. Altering the timing of delivery can cause your opponent to block at the wrong moment, opening up an otherwise tight defence.

EVADING

This term describes what the Japanese refer to as *tai-sabaki*, or body evasion. This deals in the main with fast footwork, enabling you to escape quickly by the use of rapid stepping or pivoting to attain an advantageous position whilst avoiding an opponent's charge. Also to be considered are ducking and weaving movements, which enable the upper body, and in particular the head, to be moved out of range or line of an attack whilst still being in position to counter. Great care must be taken to ensure that defence is maintained with these movements. The arms must be held ready to cover or block, especially if there is a flurry of blows. Again, it is a tactic that should be used with discretion and should immediately be followed up with an offensive action.

BLOCKING

What will become immediately apparent to the student upon engaging in free-style fighting is the apparent ineffectiveness of the basic karate blocks. You will probably never see experienced karateka in contests employing *age-uke* or *soto-uke*, for example. The reason for this is simple; there is usually not enough time to use them against an opponent who has developed karate skills to the same level as yourself. The basic blocks are powerful but they leave other parts of the body open to attack owing to their committed nature. In modern karate competition the blocking movements are usually very small and fast, and there also seems to have been a decline in the use of blocks in favour of attacking strategies.

As karate is essentially a defensive art, exemplified in Gichin Funakoshi's immortal words *'Karate ni sente nashi'* ('There is no first attack in karate'), it is quite likely that a karateka would meet an untrained attacker's assault with a powerful block. This will nullify the attack and inflict unexpected pain, so a well-executed block will serve as a good deterrent in such a situation. The practice of basic blocks along with all other basic techniques should therefore continue as an integral part of the true karateka's armoury.

Whilst the basic blocks themselves may be inappropriate for free-style sparring, they certainly lay the foundation for the more economical open-hand blocks employed because the same muscles are involved in both categories of blocks and over the years they will have become very strong and well co-ordinated. The blocks in free-style will not be as damaging, but they should still retain much of the power.

The advantage of using economical blocks for free-style is that they allow an extremely rapid recovery which in turn allows a lightening-fast counter-attack. When sparring, it is always good to acquire the habit of following your block with a counter.

Practise your blocks with a partner. Face the partner in *kamae* with your back towards a wall. Your rear foot should be positioned so that the heel just touches the wall. Now have your partner attempt to pierce your guard making repeated attacks, first with punches and then with kicks. Do not block by reaching out; block cleanly and as economically as possible, close to the target. Do not be tempted to counter-punch, although you may have a strong desire to do so. Keep your footwork to an absolute minimum. You can then progress to defending against combination attacks by having them use kicks as well as punches. The idea is to work on interpreting your partner's movement and selecting an appropriate block, not to work on escaping. The reason for positioning yourself next to the wall will soon become obvious! Ensure that you change stance during the practice so that you develop your weaker side.

FEINTING/INVITING ATTACK

This is a strategy in which you attempt to make the opponent react to an imaginary attack in order to create an opening, or draw your opponent into making a conditioned response which you have anticipated and are ready to counter. These tactics are particularly useful in 'testing' an opponent who is very 'cagey' and is content to let you attack first. Such an opponent can sometimes be tricked into attacking by offering them a target which they find difficult to resist. The trick is to provide the target in such a way that it is not an obvious invitation, or they may suspect your intention and decide not to 'bite'.

Feints are uncompleted techniques. If they are to have any effect on the opponent they must look like genuine attacks. For example, a good feint may be to raise your knee towards the opponent, as if it is your intention to kick. If the movement looks full of intention, then it is quite likely that they will react in an appropriate way by lowering their guard. To complete the strategy, you would then perhaps proceed to punch to the undefended head. Another possibility might be that having raised your knee for the front kick, you then instead convert this to a *jodan* (head-level) *mawashi-geri* (round-house kick).When using punching techniques, you would feint with one hand, but hit with the other. The possibilities are endless and should be explored. As part of your attacking strategy, feints provide a valuable tool for unlocking your opponent's weaknesses, discovering their preferred responses and style of movement.

Inviting attacks from your opponent requires courage. Rather than adopting a deliberately flawed defensive posture and awaiting your opponent's attack, which may never come, the strategy of inviting attack is a much more active approach. In this case you must attempt to engage your opponent's propensity to counter-attack. If they are highly trained and experienced, it is likely that they will be constantly poised, ready to out-time your attack or alternately block and immediately counter. Either way, you will want to encourage them to respond. Do this by planning your offence. Feint with an attack that you feel as certain as possible will result in an anticipated response. As a simple example, suppose that you attack your opponent with a feint reverse punch that looks genuine enough to elicit a downward block and reverse punch. Your initial movement will not be fully committed, enabling you strongly to block their anticipated reply and follow up with a further, but this time decisive, reverse punch.

Create your own methods by asking your partner to respond with a block and counter to your initial feints, but then block their counter and press home your 'finisher'. This kind of practice in many respects resembles *kaishi-ippon kumite* (reaction, one-step sparring), except that in that practice the first movement, instead of being a feint, is usually a committed attack. With emphasis shifted on to the initial attack, the intention is then 'all or nothing', or the concept of defeating the opponent with one blow. It is very difficult to reconcile the idea that one can be totally committed to an attack and yet have defence in mind at the same time, but that is what reaction sparring, in its proper sense, should be. When facing an experienced competitor on the mat, however, it is much more likely that you would want to test their responses by feinting and trying to draw their counter, instead of fully committing yourself to an all-out attack. In the initial stages it is probably the best strategy. Once you have ascertained the opponent's weaknesses, or the situation dictates that you are forced to take the initiative, then it is expedient to attack with full conviction and the intention to overwhelm them.

COMBINATION/SINGLE ATTACKS

Practise attack strategies using single piercing attacks, but also develop combination attacks, involving perhaps three or four rapid and consecutive hand and foot techniques. When using combinations, avoid the feeling of building up the intensity, with the intention of 'scoring' with the final technique. Such an approach implies that the initial techniques lack power or commitment, serving only as distractions for the opponent whilst you prepare to deliver the 'real' technique, and using this approach will leave you vulnerable in the early stages of your attack. Every technique in a combination should be delivered with maximum commitment to ensure that your opponent remains off balance and incapable of launching an effective counter. If the combination is diverse and contains unexpected techniques, it is quite possible to catch the opponent while they are preoccupied with trying to stay on their feet and out of your way!

VISUALIZATION

Visualization forms part of your mental preparation during training prior to competing, involving the use of your imagination. Visualization also provides an added dimension in the performance of *kata*, enabling the karateka to 'see'

their imaginary opponents and react appropriately. For many years, athletes in all fields have recognized the psychological benefits of creating mental images of themselves performing feats that they feel certain they can achieve, but which have so far eluded them. The professional boxer will 'see' himself, the challenger, standing over his floored opponent, now the ex-world champion. The high-jumper will, in their mind's eye, clear the bar and better their previous record. The tennis player, needing an ace, visualizes it to produce a service that cannot be reached.

Creating these images in the mind alleviates self-doubts and enables the athlete to approach a task with a positive attitude; but aspirations should be realistic. There is no point in visualizing yourself kicking a tall opponent on the head if you find difficulty in kicking above waist height. It is a good idea, though, to imagine yourself scoring on a superior fighter, using your favourite technique. This is the first step to actually achieving the result that you want. If you do not believe that you can do it, there is little chance of its ever happening.

To develop this skill of mental rehearsal, simply use it as often as possible. At first only picture situations well within your capability, then raise your objectives as each success is achieved. For example, prior to a grading examination, repeatedly form clear pictures of yourself performing combinations and *kata* without making any mistakes or losing your balance. Similarly, before you spar, create in your mind an image of yourself pressing home a successful counter-attack. You will find that these positive images have a habit of fulfilling themselves. Gradually, this mental conditioning will become an integral part of your training, providing the necessary link between the psyche and the physical.

YOUR OPPONENT'S STYLE

Unless you have seen your opponent compete previously, you may have no idea how they fight. They may be, broadly speaking, a defender or an attacker, a kicker or a puncher. These stereotypes were much more prevalent in years gone by; today there is emerging a new type of competitor, proficient in all areas and able to mask their weaknesses behind a determined, resolute attitude. Prepare yourself for as many eventualities as possible and ensure that you develop your armoury and tactics to give your opponent as many problems as you can. Whoever your opponent is, it should be your intention to make their life very difficult indeed for those two minutes that the match lasts.

YOUR MENTAL ATTITUDE

You must cultivate a strong, determined attitude just prior to competing. Having utilized visualization skills in the run-up to the competition, you should now not concentrate on trying to use a specific technique because this interferes with your ability to respond intuitively. Go on to the mat with the intention of doing your very best, but without focusing on winning; concern about winning is about looking into the future and distracts the mind from the present moment. All your attention should be on the task that faces you at that precise moment and not the possible outcome of a match. This is where the teachings of Zen are directly applicable to *shiai*, the contest.

If you dwell on victory or defeat, you will not be able to attain *zanshin*. Intellectual processes should be suspended; you should not think, but let your mind be empty and calm. As you bow to your opponent and the match begins, you must be ready to abort any strategy you have in mind in favour of an instinctive response. It pays not to be too rigid, but to have a flexible and receptive mind – just be patient and see what happens. React honestly, directly and without hesitation. When you see the opportunity, seize it and give everything. If, in that moment, you are defeated, then you will have no cause for regret. On the other hand, if you are successful, do not become too excited, but remain calm and prepare yourself for the next round.

9 THE KARATE COMPETITION

There are two distinct types of competition: *kata* and *kumite*. Within these two spheres are many categories, divided by age and gender. These are further subdivided into individual and team events. This book is concerned with preparation for individual *kumite* competition. Having practised the skills we have described, you will probably want to test them in actual competition, but be guided by your club instructor as to when you are ready for this. *Kumite* carries with it the risk of injury, so to minimize this risk, it is essential that both competitors are able to perform karate to a high standard.

It is important to equip yourself with a good mouthguard, which is compulsory, and a groin guard or chest guard, as appropriate, which is highly recommended. Regularly train with these protective devices so that you become used to them. Paying attention to this sort of detail beforehand allows you to concentrate totally on your karate on the day of the competition.

Children's events will be subdivided into height categories and there are also separate competitions for lower and higher grades. Juniors, aged 16 to 21, also have a separate event from the adults, usually respectfully referred to as 'seniors', so the number of permutations can surprise the novice. The competition takes the form of a number of rounds, only the winners of each round going on to the next one. In a competition of any size, the initial rounds take place simultaneously on several marked areas. These areas are usually marked out for both the *kata* and *kumite* events and will be approximately 8 m square (86ft square). In the centre, about 3 m (10ft) apart, will be two short parallel lines, which indicate the starting positions for the two fighters.

Competitions usually begin with the team *kumite* and then the individual event, followed by *kata*. Posted in a prominent position will be many sheets containing lists of names of all the competitors and their categories. Check well in advance that your name is in the expected category and note the sheet number that your name appears on, because competitors are summoned to areas according to this number. The list will provide you with information such as how many competitors are in your particular pool, and whom you will meet in the first round. You will be able to ascertain the number of rounds you will have to survive to reach the finals and also whether you have a 'bye'; that is, a first round in which you are not matched with an opponent, and therefore automatically go through to the second. This situation arises when there are insufficient numbers to enable everyone to be matched.

Frank Brennan and Ronnie Christopher provided capacity crowds with many heart-stopping moments in countless 'showdowns', before Frank's retirement in 1992.

When your sheet number is called, you will be directed to one of the numbered fighting areas. The names will be read out to confirm that all competitors are present. You then all line up at the edge of the fighting area and the chief referee then conducts the formal bowing ceremony which precedes the competition. You will then be instructed to sit down at the edge of the fighting area in readiness for your bout.

You may have to wait some time for your turn to fight, so use this time constructively by watching closely other fighters in the pool, particularly those whom you may have to face. Often a basic strategy can be devised to cope with an opponent just by observing their preferred techniques or fighting style. For example, you might see that a particular fighter is winning by countering very effectively with *gyaku-zuki*, or overwhelming their opponents with a flurry of techniques. In the first case, you would be wise to use the strategies described in the section on feinting and inviting attack. In the second, you might use evasion, *tai-sabaki*.

When you are called up to fight, either you or your opponent will be given a red belt to wear so that the referees can distinguish between the fighters. Move to the fighting line as directed by the referee.

You will then be instructed to bow to your opponent, *'rei'*. On the instruction *'hajime'*, you begin the match. You must instantly stop fighting on the command *'yame'*, stop; or *'soremade'*, end of match.

There are two systems of refereeing, the 'mirror system' where there are two referees, one standing to either side of the competitors, and the 'judge system', where there is one referee and a judge sits at each corner of the fighting area. The object of having the additional referee is to ensure that every scoring technique will be visible to at least one person. Elimination rounds are usually refereed using the mirror system whilst the finals would be conducted with the four corner judges. Having the judges means that usually at least two people will have seen a technique, which can be important if a result is disputed. The judges communicate with the referee both verbally and by signalling with a pair of flags.

There will also be other officials involved with the match: the time-keeper and a person recording the results will sit at a nearby table and there will also be an official arbitrator in case of a disputed result. Match regulations require that when there is a disputed result, complaints are not made directly by the competitor to any of the judges, but are passed through the team manager, or club instructor, to the arbitrator.

The referee has sole command over the match. He announces the start, when to halt or restart, when a point is scored and when the match is ended. *Ippon* would be awarded for a decisive technique, or *waza-ari* for one lacking in some small degree. The referee also has the power to issue warnings, to dismiss or suspend a contestant from the match, to obtain advice from the judges, to decide victory by a casting vote in the event of a tie and to extend the duration of a match to obtain a result. It will become increasingly clear that responding to the referee comes second only to coping with your opponent.

You win by scoring *ippon*; two *waza-ari* count as an *ippon*. Matches may be decided either on this single score, *ippon shobu*, or by scoring three times, *sanbon shobu*. You can lose by a foul or disqualification. The scoring areas are the head and neck, the chest and abdomen, and the back. Techniques delivered to anywhere else, other than the arms and legs, are illegal. Attacks to the groin, the hip joint, knee or instep will result in disqualification, as will persistent attacks to the shin, grabbing and clinching or dangerous throws. Allowable techniques are punches, kicks and closed-fist strikes. A legal technique to a legal target will be disallowed, or even counted as a foul, if it is uncontrolled and causes damage to the opponent, so-called 'excessive contact'.

In addition to the techniques you use, you must also consider space and time. Any technique delivered outside the match area is invalid. So a competitor with a foot over the line cannot defend themselves and anyone near the edge of the area is constrained in the response they can make. Repeatedly stepping outside the area will result in disqualification. Normally a match lasts for two minutes, although it is common for finals of a competition to be of three minutes' duration. The referee can add to this time, up to a limit of five minutes, or hold extra two-minute rounds with breaks in between, in order to obtain a result. You have to prepare yourself to fight effectively over this period of time. You should be aware that the time-keeper will sound a bell 30 seconds before the scheduled end of the match. If you are trailing at this point, perhaps you should think of an all-or-nothing attack, and if you are in the lead, be aware that your opponent may try this strategy.

It is generally understood that for the referee to award an *ippon*, the technique must be exact, effective and powerful. That means good form, good attitude, vigour, *zanshin*, as well as proper timing and correct distancing; summed up as good karate technique. However, some deviation from the ideal may still qualify for an *ippon* under certain conditions, as, for example, if a counter-attack actually pre-empts the opponent's attack, so that the moment the attacker begins their move they are neutralized and countered. Another example would be a good counter-attack delivered from a potentially disastrous position, such as being momentarily off balance from a sweep, or an instant before stepping outside the area; snatching victory from the jaws of defeat. A combination of successive attacks or combined use of a kick and punch or sweep and punch is also more likely to score *ippon* than a single technique. For this reason it pays to develop defensive strategies that prevent your opponent delivering successive techniques. Should your opponent actually turn away from a determined attack, as can happen in novice matches, or momentarily drop their defences, then almost any attack will score. Similarly, if you manage to catch a kick or punch, or your opponent falls for any reason, you must *immediately* step in and deliver an effective attack.

If the match ends without the score of *ippon* in favour of one person, or a foul or disqualification against the other, then the decision will rest on whether there has been a *waza-ari*, whether there has been an official warning for a foul, the number of escapes outside the area, or even the comparative fighting vigour and attitude, the technical skill and strategy displayed or the number of attacking moves made.

Novices to competition often fail to win not because they lack karate skills but because they do not understand the implications of the competition rules. The most common mistakes are to deliver a technique from those crucial two or three inches too far away, to make excessive contact or to move outside the area. Remember to train so that techniques are delivered from a realistic distance and pulled off the target at the instant that contact is made. To deliver a fast, powerful technique in a split second of opportunity, such as a round-house kick to the head that neither just fails to connect nor has excessive contact, requires an immense amount of skill and training. To score with such speed, precision and control is a real achievement, gives immense satisfaction and is the real objective of competition karate.

10 FITNESS AND MOBILITY

The cornerstones of fitness are flexibility, strength and circulo-respiratory efficiency. Flexibility is that element of fitness which is concerned with maximizing the range of motion of joints. The repertoire of techniques used in karate can be particularly demanding on flexibility. Strength is measured by the force of contraction exerted by a muscle and as it is the muscular system that supports and moves the body, strength needs to be developed in such a way that it provides protection against stress injuries and allows for powerful, explosive movements. Circulo-respiratory efficiency is the ability of the heart, blood vessels and lungs to function effectively with increased demand, transporting oxygen to the tissues and removing waste products, and when developed, provides the athlete with aerobic endurance.

All these aspects of fitness are developed to a degree through regular, hard karate training, but to promote a higher level of fitness, the concept of 'overload' is applied to exercise. The principle behind this is that gradually increasing the demands on the body will trigger it into developing the strength and circulo-respiratory capability appropriate to these new demands. The rate of increase should be carefully controlled because overtraining – making too much of a demand too soon – will cause damage. Recovering from training injuries will slow down your development. The body is a marvellous biological machine which, if properly cared for, will not wear out with use but actually becomes stronger.

In struggling to find the correct form, novices expend more energy than advanced grades when performing the same movements. This means that beginners may make gains in fitness that elude higher grades. In many cases a 'plateau' of fitness is reached by the advanced karateka which may well not be high enough to meet the demands of competition. A competitor may have to fight and perform *kata* in many rounds throughout the course of the day, which requires a high level of stamina and endurance.

Even without the demands of competition, karateka should be concerned with developing a level of fitness above the routine demands of dojo training. Not all classes are particularly demanding in a physical sense. For example, the instructor may spend considerable time on developing technical points as opposed to just making the students sweat. You should develop a range of flexibility in the hips that exceeds that required for the high kicks, so as to provide a safety margin against the possibility of self-injury. The muscles, tendons and ligaments should be strengthened to withstand the stress caused by dynamic, vigorous action. Similarly, aerobic capacity should be increased so that maximum effort can be sustained for longer periods. Improved endurance helps prevent a loss of speed and quality of technique towards the end of a match, particularly if the time is extended. The fitter competitor will have the advantage in this situation.

What follows is an introduction to the methods for promoting the three elements of fitness: flexibility, strength and circulo-respiratory efficiency.

FLEXIBILITY AND STRETCHING

Contrary to popular belief, just performing karate techniques, including the high kicks, will not in itself increase suppleness significantly. Without a comprehensive stretching routine, the karateka will at best only maintain their existing range of motion, which may be less than desirable. Being flexible, particularly in the hips and lower limbs, provides an enormous advantage over the less supple karateka in the practice of extended kicking techniques. It is now recognized that an increase in flexibility provides the athlete with the scope for improved performance and a reduction in stress-related injuries. 'Range of motion' describes the extent to which joints can be moved without injury. This includes an *active range* in which positions can be attained using voluntary muscular contraction and, beyond this, a *passive range* in which the limbs are moved to their natural limit with the assistance of an outside force. There are passive and active stretching methods which can modify these ranges.

The active range of motion provides the scope for karateka to kick without overstretching the muscles. Ideally this active range of motion should match the skill requirements for high kicks. It is the range within which full voluntary muscular control can be exerted. Beyond the limit of the active range lies the passive range. To move a limb into this range requires an outside force. This can be achieved by swinging a limb in a ballistic manner through the active range until the momentum takes it into the passive range. However, the nearer to a joint's natural limit that a limb is forced, the higher the risk of injury. As muscle strength declines nearing the joint's limit, momentum is halted only by the resilience of the soft tissues. Should these tissues not be conditioned to withstand such abuse, injury becomes almost inevitable. Young children and older adults are particularly vulnerable to injury in this manner. To reduce this danger, novice karateka who fall into these categories are advised to kick only within their active range of motion.

The proven best method for increasing the passive range of motion in a safe, controlled way is by solitary slow and static stretching (S&SS), in which exercises are performed in a series of progressive, relaxed positions, with the subject always being in control. A passive stretch is applied by allowing the muscles to relax as much as possible whilst the limb is taken to the limit of its movement. For example, if you sit on the floor and spread your legs as far apart as possible, you can achieve a passive stretch by grasping one of your legs and using your arms to move it out so as to increase the stretch. For the best results, you should try to remain in this position for at least 30 seconds. In this period of time the muscles and connective tissues (dense fibrous sheets of tissue that join other tissues together) slowly stretch, and it will then be possible to move the leg a little further. By repeating this process, you will come to the point where further movement cannot be obtained. Remain in this final position for at least 30 seconds. As muscles, tendons and connective tissues become conditioned, it will be possible to remain in the maximal position for much longer periods, with benefit.

This form of stretching does not require great effort, just plenty of time and a relaxed approach. With any form of stretching, it is important to perform the exercises exactly as described so as to stretch the correct muscles. Do not approach stretching in a competitive spirit, straining yourself trying to emulate the performance of others with greater flexibility. This defeats the purpose of the exercises and risks injury.

Within the active range, you stretch in an 'active' way by contracting muscles to move a limb as far as you can and then hold it there for ten seconds. Now relax for a few moments. Repeat this pattern a number of times, and each time it should be possible to move the limb a fraction further, until fatigue sets in. As the maximal position is reached, with the muscles tensing hard, the exercise will become isometric in nature. This describes exercise where full muscular effort is applied without any resulting movement. The body's natural response to this situation is to bring more muscle fibres into action to overcome what is interpreted as a resistance to movement. This form of exercise increases strength at the limit of active movement.

Normally, a muscle exerts most force at about the mid-range of the movement it controls. By increasing the strength at the end of the range, the speed and control of techniques is enhanced, particularly the high kicks. The static step-by-step kicking methods detailed at the close of Chapter 7 use precisely this method. This demonstrates how you should always endeavour to build the appropriate strength along with flexibility.

The concept of 'specificity' is important in that static methods of stretching, the types described so far, should as far as possible mimic the movements actually performed in karate. Practising karate kicks at full speed and power promotes a different kind of flexibility, called dynamic flexibility. This kind of flexibility can be demonstrated by considering a roundhouse kick performed very slowly and then at speed. The height that you can reach when moving slowly demonstrates your active range of flexibility. The extra height that you would obtain if a partner raised your leg whilst the kick was fully extended demonstrates your passive range of flexibility. In between these two limits is a range where, when the kick is made at speed, the momentum of the leg carries it past the active range but, most importantly, the muscles can still control the limb so that you can perform an accurate technique and pull it off the target. So whilst static methods of stretching will increase overall range of motion, the dynamic movements, such as in the high kicks, are what makes flexibility gains useful and functional.

The EKGB-approved warm-up routine consists of exercises specifically relevant to karate and to which S&SS can be applied. You may already be familiar with them, but to use these exercises as a stretching routine, you will need to perform them more slowly, holding the positions for longer, than is usual in a class warm-up. The method is simple and straightforward:

1. Thoroughly warm up by running on the spot, doing squat thrusts and any other combination of similar aerobic-style exercises to increase the heartbeat and respiration. This will produce heat, which raises the temperature of the deep muscle and connective tissues to be stretched. Exertion should not be such that you become breathless, a slight perspiration being a good indication that you are ready to stretch. Should you feel as though you are cooling down during the stretching exercises, repeat some or all of the warm-up again. The important thing is to *keep* warm.

2. To stretch in the S&SS method, go through each of the positions in your regular pre-training dojo warm-up in the usual systematic manner for an all-over stretch. For example, work from head to toe and in a balanced way by performing positions both left and right.

Avoid ballistic-style movements, those in which limbs are swung loosely without muscular control. This kind of movement is potentially damaging, especially when moving joints near to the limits of their movement; also, take care to ensure that joints are properly aligned to avoid damaging them.

Movements that specifically stretch ligaments are dangerous as they can affect joint stability. Ligaments are the fibrous tissues that hold the bones together at the joints, and the knee is particularly vulnerable.

When performing stretching exercises it is best to work alone because partner-assisted stretching can be hazardous if your partner is unfamiliar with the exercises or is unaware of your limitations. The important thing is that you remain in control of the stretch. Do not rush, but try to relax completely and *allow* your body to slowly stretch. Come out of each stretch smoothly and slowly and remember to breath naturally.

3. Do not perform any movements that involve the body in unsupported leaning. For example, leaning backwards without support can hyperextend the spine and significantly increase the risk of damage. Be careful when twisting, turning and rolling the neck by avoiding rapid, jerky and unnatural planes of movement.

4. Immediately after you have completed the S&SS exercises, your body will be ready for the more demanding active stretching, which will then provide even greater gains in strength and usable flexibility.

KIME AND BALLISTIC AND DYNAMIC MOVEMENT

Karate technique is composed of ballistic and dynamic movement. A kick, block, punch or strike is typified by a dynamic origin, in which the muscles contract rapidly to cause an explosive initial movement. As momentum is increased and full speed attained, the muscles largely shut down, and are as relaxed as possible to allow a ballistic-style movement. But as the target is struck or, as in basics, when the limb is about to extend fully, the muscles are again brought into play to contract rapidly and so activate *kime*.

You get a sharp reminder that you have failed to employ *kime* if your kick inadvertently misses the target, especially if kicking with full power at a heavy bag or kick-shield. Without the usual 'trigger' of contact, the leg continues in a ballistic manner until the tissues surrounding the joints reach their limit and are abruptly and painfully forced to absorb the shock as the leg is locked out.

When practising basics, you cannot trigger *kime* with contact, because the stimulus is absent, but you utilize and develop the body's natural reflex action of tensing muscles just short of full extension, the point at which power is usually released in karate techniques.

DEVELOPING STRENGTH

A judoka will spend a considerable amount of time in developing strength because this has great benefits when engaging in *randori*, the judo equivalent of karate free-sparring. Although the use of strength is not so obvious in karate, it does provide the basis for the speed and power necessary for the techniques to be effective.

Many people who devote themselves to karate find that they simply do not have enough time to go to a gym and lift weights. Without doubt, 'pumping iron' is the proven best way to build muscles and strength. If you have the time to pursue both disciplines then that is fine, but it may not be possible. Fortunately, a great deal of useful strength building and conditioning exercises can be done with little or no equipment and in a minimum of time.

The active stretching exercises that have been described will develop the strength of the legs in a way specifically suited for the kicks. Deep knee bends and lunges will further develop the legs. Push-ups can be done in a variety of ways to develop the arms, chest, shoulders and upper body. Sit-ups can develop the whole abdominal region but must be performed properly, with knees bent and lower spine kept in contact with the floor. The student will be able to find other examples in books on fitness and exercise. Apply the 'overload' principle by performing more repetitions or by increasing the difficulty of the exercise. For example, when performing push-ups you can elevate your feet, or when doing sit-ups, you can use any household object which has some weight and can be clasped in front of the chest. You should include this kind of exercise in your daily training routine.

DEVELOPING ENDURANCE

It is possible to be strong or to be flexible without actually being fit, because the basis of fitness is aerobic endurance. Aerobic means 'with air' and refers to vigorous activities that are maintained for long periods, and therefore require fresh oxygen from the bloodstream to provide the energy needed by the muscles. To develop this capability, you have to build up the circulo-respiratory system and to do this, you have to sustain a vigorous activity for a minimum of 20 minutes.

Karate training involves explosive activity of short duration. A typical class might last one to two hours but the action occurs in short, intensive bursts that allow for recovery in between. The muscular and nervous systems benefit from this type of training, but the circulo-respiratory system is practically unaffected. The only way to make the training into an aerobic activity is to reduce the periods of rest and prolong the periods of activity so that the heart rate does not drop significantly for at least 20 minutes. If karate is practised in this way, twice per week, then aerobic capacity will be improved. You should consider setting aside extra time for fitness and conditioning exercise, particularly if regular dojo training is not consistently physically demanding. The competition karateka is an athlete, and like all athletes needs to be fully fit.